WHAT IS CANADA?

A wolf in sheep's clothing,
or the leader in new progress?

A YOUTH PERSPECTIVE

GARETH CHANTLER

Note for Librarians: A cataloguing record for this book is available from Library and Archives Canada at www.collectionscanada.ca/amicus/index-e.html

ISBN 1-4120-8440-7

Printed in Victoria, BC, Canada. Printed on paper with minimum 30% recycled fibre.
Trafford's print shop runs on "green energy" from solar, wind and other environmentally-friendly power sources.

TRAFFORD
PUBLISHING™
Offices in Canada, USA, Ireland and UK

Book sales for North America and international:
Trafford Publishing, 6E–2333 Government St.,
Victoria, BC V8T 4P4 CANADA
phone 250 383 6864 (toll-free 1 888 232 4444)
fax 250 383 6804; email to orders@trafford.com
Book sales in Europe:
Trafford Publishing (UK) Limited, 9 Park End Street, 2nd Floor
Oxford, UK OX1 1HH UNITED KINGDOM
phone 44 (0)1865 722 113 (local rate 0845 230 9601)
facsimile 44 (0)1865 722 868; info.uk@trafford.com
Order online at:
trafford.com/06-0195

10 9 8 7 6 5 4 3 2

Acknowledgements

I would like to thank everyone who had a hand in my writing of this book. There were many people who I bounced ideas off in conversation, whether they knew it or not, and often their thoughts and (offhand) answers inspired me to write more, cover more basis, and generally elucidate my ideas. So to everyone who I grew up with, went to school with, swam in the same pool with, or spent a summer with, thanks. I would also like to thank those who took some time to read over early drafts of chapters one and two, offering valuable suggestions. These people, by reading and commenting on these two chapters, helped shape my editing goals for the whole book. Without their time and input, this book would not have been possible without any formal editor. Thank you, Tessa Young, MA Rowe, Crystal Xiao, my sister Aylish, Dan Imbrogno, Braden Brinkman, Steph Latella, Stacey Xu, and Roshan Sethi. Special thanks go to Tessa Young for helping me organize my research and notes, and Laura Pomeroy for helping me with presentation ideas. I would like to especially thank my parents for purchasing the laptop with which I wrote this book. I would also like to thank them for allowing me to form my own opinions and for never offering or imposing their own ideas unless asked. This lack of interference is a big reason why I think the way I do. Finally I would like to thank all those who see the value in empowering and educating (though the two are very similar) youth in the world, namely my previous good teachers and coaches, the staff of Shad Valley, and Canadians like Craig Kielburger and Raffi.

– Gareth Chantler, August 2005

Conventions

The term 'equality' is used in this book. Let the reader be sure this refers to the notion of equality in life's opportunity, free from discrimination, as well as the ubiquitous possession of fundamental human rights. This is opposed to the absolute equality of condition in life's experience. Terms such as 'blacks', 'whites', 'pro-life', and 'pro-choice' can be also found throughout the book, in quotes, because the author believes that these are fictional and unnecessary terms. Nonetheless these terms exist in the real world, and when one discusses something like discrimination and affirmative action that both rely on a belief in terms such as 'blacks' and 'whites', their use is inevitable. Real world solutions have to understand real world concepts, however fallacious they are. Most endnotes are references to a source of information, but may the reader note that some are more detailed explanations of a concept, or an elaboration of a story. The author is fully responsible for the contents of this book, as both the writer and editor. I am sure there are many small errors and perhaps a few larger ones. Any inaccuracies are a result of the author's oversight alone.

Contents

Preface: A Youth Perspective vii

One: Is Canada: Searching for a National Identity
or Eschewing One? 1

Two: Political Mindset: Post Modern Democracy 8

Three: Canadian Society: Contemporary Change and Complacency 34

Four: Canada's Foreign Policy: Aspiring Middle Power or
Inspiring World Peace? 47

Five: The Environment: Sustainability, sustainability everywhere,
and still the air stinks 79

Conclusion: What is the future of Canada? 114

Endnotes 117

Appendix: 132

Preface
A Youth Perspective

Young people are the most disenfranchised group in the world. Most often they have no say in the decisions of their country and no vote in who makes them. They are the segment of the population with the least responsibility and in parallel, the least power. This characteristic creates a simple dynamic: youth are often helpless. When a society thrives, it invests in its youth, providing a safe and healthy environment for their development. Youth are then (often unwitting) recipients of success. When a society fails, the first victims are those who are innocent. Many people are born each day. Whether one is born in North America or Africa, into opulence or destitution, into a childhood of schooling or soldiering, is a dice roll.

Infants, children, and teenagers are society's most valuable assets. Youth are the connection to the future; an investment in the well being of a society's youth is an investment in the world's future well being. Policy that understands this relation is hard to find: few countries covet youth in such a way. The opposite is often true; the young are seen as dead weight.

As a youth develops, he or she often either adopts the ideology of his or her guardian(s) or rebels against it. When neither of these complexes occur, a youth's disenfranchisement in society often grants a perspective that is particularly objective (if naïve). When compared with youth, those powerful or entrenched in society often possess a narrow domain of what they consider to be possible. Youth seldom regard legal machinations and political realism, the pushing and pulling of labour and capital, government posturing and selling out, or the popularity of ideology. Simply put, youth think problems have solutions. Without perceiving an interest (monetary or otherwise) in an issue's outcome, a youth's solutions are often imagined objectively. Without an inhibited notion of the possible, these solutions appear in the form of comprehensive cures, as opposed to assuaging remedies, and involve disregarding an assumption considered by those older to be the starting point of discussion.

Being closely connected to the future and possessing little in the way of perceived boundaries, youth understandably view the world in different ways from their older, 'real-world' counterparts. Consequently this unique perspective leads to a unique set of priorities, interests and ideas. The following chapters detail one of these perspectives and imply from what assumptions it formed. This book is not about how every youth views Canada. This book is about how one person, at one point in their youth, views Canada.

I have tried to strike a balance: the book is meant to be both accessible and appealing, including background while still provoking reflection. Perhaps the fact that the opinion being expressed is from an age bracket seldom heard from, will add to the reader's interest. Some characteristics of a youth opinion I have outlined – such as an interest in the future's well-being or an enhanced belief in the possible – I believe have lead me to this unique perspective, one that is marginalized in Canadian discourse for obvious, some would argue inherent, reasons. Obviously one of the goals is to answer the question posed in the title. At times the topic selection may seem eclectic, perhaps diversionary from the title: the reader should be wary of this idea. Young people are the most disenfranchised group in the world. In addition to answering the question posed, I hope this book also contributes a small part in the enfranchising and engaging of Canadian youth. If nothing else, I will be able to later reflect and realize in entirety why the voting age should be where it is, if not older.

1

Is Canada:
Searching for a National Identity or Eschewing One?

"Until we stop fighting that war between France and Britain circa 1759, we will never see an "identity revolution" befitting the country's demographic evolution. Put more bluntly, until the core questions of nationality have been resolved, everything else will be secondary." [1]

– Naomi Klein

"Canada will be a strong country when Canadians of all provinces feel at home in all parts of the country, and when they feel that all Canada belongs to them."

– Pierre Elliot Trudeau

Oh Canada: our home and *native* land.

Or as political science professors Michael Ornstein and H. Michael Stevenson assert: "The Canadian state established in 1867 can be characterized as an attempt by indigenous capitalist interests to establish a hegemonic project for the economic development of a colonial society threatened by changes in the international and imperial system of which it was a subordinate part." [2]

That certainly seems to have been true at the time. Canada, like America in 1776 was the creation of rich white men trying to *capitalize*. In contrast to his American counterparts though, Sir John A. Macdonald, Canada's 'founding father', was not a majestic man with a genius, epiphanic vision of Canada's future. Most Canadians do not revere him – he did not shape Canada into what it is today. He was a stepping stone in a sequence of events, an important part of history.

Canada was an English colony – originally a French colony before that. And before that, it was the land of the First Nations, the Huron, Blackfoot, Onondaga and Mi'kmaq. It wasn't called Canada back when the Iroquois were slaughtering the Huron, or the English the French on the Plains of Abraham.

Canada was definitely called simply Canada when the papers where signed by Sir John A. in 1867. That was the beginning of Canada, as we know it.

So what is Canada now? Surely it is not still the place Ornstein and Stevenson describe, whose sole purpose since inception has been a resource based society economically and politically dominated by rich white males ("indigenous capitalistic interests"). Canada has multiculturalism and bilingualism. Canada is a nation of all peoples, devoid of racial segregation, where women can vote. Canada is one of the best countries around: responsible and committed to the peace and prosperity of its people and the world, while holding hands and singing songs.

As clearly as this is true, then at some point in between 1867 and 2005, Canada must have changed: morphed into the peace loving, tree hugging, industrious, profitable-to-all, multicultural utopia that it is. Let us brainstorm and pin down when this occurred....

Was it...

...when Canada sheltered poor formerly-enslaved 'blacks' via the Underground Railroad from their southern oppressors?

Or was it when Canada had separate towns built (usually in mud) for 'blacks' in Nova Scotia?

...when Canada finished constructing the National Dream, a railway that stretched from coast to coast, uniting the whole country?

Or was it when Canada exploited migrant Chinese workers, killing 'one for every mile of railroad', in order to construct the National Dream, finally completing it in 1885?

...when Canada passed the Chinese Exclusion Act of 1923, limiting Chinese immigration in an attempt to maintain 'ethnic purity'?

Or was it when Canada repealed the Chinese Exclusion Act in 1947?

...when Canada went to fight in WWI, losing 66 655[3] men as a pawn for British imperialistic goals, to fight German and Austrian imperialistic goals?

Or was it when Canada renamed Bond, Ontario: Kingston during WWI?

...when in 1917 Canada finally gave some[4] women the right to vote after they had come out of the kitchen and into the factories to facilitate the country's conversion into a giant military industrial complex?

Or was it when Canada granted all women suffrage?

... when 42,042[5] Canadians were killed in WWII?

Or was it during WWII, when Canada placed 21000 Japanese Canadians in internment camps?

...when Canada sent 512 men to die in Korea in 1950?

Or was it when Canada forced First Nation children to speak only English?

...when Canada let a hysterical fear of Stalinist Communism silence thoughts and paralyze actions as the United States first invaded Vietnam in 1959? Or tried to invade Cuba in 1963? Or bombed Cambodia in 1969? Or attacked Nicaragua in 1983? Or funded Osama Bin Laden in 1979? Or Saddam Hussein in 1980?

Or when Canada sheepishly said nothing, as America bombed Sudan in 1998? Or bombed Kosovo in 1999? No, Canada also dropped bombs. Or bombed and invaded Afghanistan in 2002? No wait, Canada sent troops to Afghanistan...

Was it when Canada did not sent troops to Iraq in 2003?

It must have been then.

Canada, for all its splendours, does not have a clean slate of history. 'Black' Canadians did not always have the same rights as 'white' Canadians. Women were not always, in the eyes of the law, equal to men. Though now the ink of the law claims women and men enjoy equality, they do not in the blind eyes of the economy. A study in 1999, found that in Canada for every dollar the average man makes, the average woman makes 80 cents[6]. Minorities were oppressed a lot in Canadian history: First Nations, French Canadians, Jewish-Canadians, Ukrainian-Canadians, homosexuals, women, Sikhs, Muslims, Hindus, Protestants, Catholics, Pacifists, on and on. The list of those wronged in Canada is long. And while the history of the United States is littered with the horrible, Canadian citizens must realize that Canadian history has its own egregious events which greatly influence present realities.

Canadians and Americans alike often criticize contemporary America, referencing its violent history as a cause for its current deficiencies. When this comparison is made, a better quality of life in Canada – less gun violence, better health care – is often alluded to. Even if the magnitudes of violence in respective histories differ, what does that really impart? Does it mean that the 152 gun homicides in Canada in 2002, compared to over 11,000 in the US, are justified, or should be disregarded? It seems that Canadians often focus on quality by comparison. Should Canadians be complacent in the way in which they live their lives? Should they think that as a first world country, they are impervious to real world problems? That their current society is ideal or good enough because of the state of the rest of the world? Perhaps in addition to Canadians saying "I am thankful I live in Canada" they could also say "Let us make Canada even better".

If I were asked to help facilitate the thinking of Canadians who believe that their country is perfect by comparison, I would draw my own comparison. During the Cold War, the American population believed they were in the right: that their system of beliefs was moral, while the system of beliefs of the United Soviet Socialist Republic was immoral. Often this opinion was reinforced when they looked to the unjustifiable oppression of the poor and the death from starvation that Stalin wilfully wrought upon his own people. Sometimes this led to faith in perfection by comparison, with confidence that 'the ends justify the means'. Once this ideology took root during the Cold War, the call to eradicate the evil of 'Communism' led to all kinds of injustice. These included the kind of domestic fear mongering typified by McCarthyism and the House Committee of Un-American activities. Censorship of freedom of speech and the arts prevailed, most famously in Hollywood blacklisting. This ideology also included rationalizing terrible 'proxy' wars in places like Korea (1950-53) and Vietnam (1959-1975). Finally, it also provided justification for espionage campaigns such as the unsuccessful Bay of Pigs invasion (1963), and the overthrow of the democratically elected government of Iran in favour of a dictator (1953). Those gripped by this ideology look back and say that 'Communism' (not Stalinism or Totalitarianism) had to be defeated, based on the aggression and evilness of the USSR. Often cited are hostile actions such as the 1979 invasion of Afghanistan by the USSR. But does this 'perfection by comparison' rationalize the funding of Osama Bin Laden in 1979 by the United States, to drive back the Soviets?

Canadians are often lulled into the misconception that Canada could not be better, regardless of standing in comparison to others. Though grievances may be arguably less, let the American experience be instructive. The scale of differences between Canada and the United States is less severe than those found in the Cold War between the United States and USSR. But a lesson can still be learned: Canada may be the country people most want to live in, but it is not the country people should want. Canada is not a finished product.

What should Canada be? How do the people form and shape that Canada; put the country on the path towards what is ideal? Canada is clearly not still the place that was founded as a capitalist enterprise back in 1867, and yet the imprints of that legacy can still be seen today. Canada is even further removed in time from the Plains of Abraham, but the conflict between France and England over Canada left residue that nearly destroyed the country as recently as the 1980 and 1995 separatist referendums. People seem to always be talking about what it means to be Canadian, and other people complain that being Canadian is too often described as how people are not American.

Some say that being Canadian now (a modern Canadian) has something to do with multiculturalism, it is no longer about being a settler from England, or Europe, as it once was. Others decry that multiculturalism breeds a type of cultural segregation: that communities don't mix. That Hindu-Canadians don't interact with Muslim-Canadians – they live in the same city – but in separate parts of town. That people therefore consider themselves Irish, Japanese or Columbian first, before they consider themselves Canadian: even if they were born and lived their whole lives in Canada. The argument is that if Canada developed a national identity, then it would be more efficient and cohesive, its citizens confident in a collective identity. On the other side, people hear this and alarm bells go off, thinking that these people who wish all to have a common vision on what a Canadian should be about are anti-ethnicity or anti-immigration. Should Canada even have a national identity? Naomi Klein writes about "the strange arbitrariness of nationality"[7] and yet in the same essay the quote beginning this chapter is found.

National identity seems to be *the* question for Canada, wreaking havoc across the land, spurring referendums, and alienating the first/second/ad infinitum generation of immigrants. Mel Hurtig, self described 'Canadian Nationalist', kicks and screams about Canada being destroyed by Americanization. In *Vanishing Country* he quotes Steven Pearlstein with significant alarm, "Economically, culturally, socially, demographically, even politically, Canadians say [Canada] is becoming indistinguishable from the U.S."[8] But if Canadians do not have a common identity in the first place, what is there to lose?

What is a nation?

It seems to me that in the past the definition of a nation came from the appearance of the people, their religion, and their language. Italians spoke Italian, were dark haired, and worshipped Roman Catholicism. This definition is no longer true. As immigration and globalization turn countries into melodies of religions, ethnicities and languages, the old definition of nationhood does not hold up. There is at least one country that seems to have developed a new definition. Robert Cooper writes:

> Following their experiences in the twentieth century, most European states have become less nationalist, while America has not. Perhaps this is partly because European nationalism has been associated with ethnicity, whereas American nationalism is defined by loyalty to the constitution, making it easier to preserve in a more diverse society.[9]

Ideological nationalism: that doesn't sound too bad. Some argue that is what Canada should be about, with the condition that the ideology should be one that is different from that of the Untied States. In fact, it seems that is what the Liberal Party, or its branding, claims it is all about: a Canada that is based on the ideology of the Charter of Rights and Freedoms, encouraging multiculturalism and ensuring minority rights, peace, and stability. Others contest that Canada already has a national identity, albeit a mild one. Rudyard Griffiths writes: "Canada's civic culture has long been marked by powerful interest in institutions and the programs they deliver as the embodiment of the values we share."[10] John Godfrey and Rob Mclean concur: "a nationality is precisely defined by its social programs. That is, a nationality is defined by its perception of the mutual obligations that exist among members of a society, how those obligations are articulated through the political process, and how they are communicated through the arts, literature, and popular culture."[11] So is Canada's national identity based on what it has accomplished in the realm of social institutions? Griffiths explains that this is another way of not being American:

> Unlike our southern neighbour, and in order to be unlike it, we es-chewed a national identity founded on a set of ideological principles. Our great political accomplishments – the means through which we articulated our political and civic values – came to be understood in institutional terms.[12]

A national identity based on hospitals and schools? That does not sound very powerful or inspiring. Conrad Black tersely regards this reasoning as mythical: "A nationality cannot define itself by its social programs."[13] Can Canadians not embrace a higher calling? It sounds romantic. Do we wish to become patriots of Canada as Americans are of America? When put in that context most would say no, but when more subtle, it appears some people have convinced themselves that is what we need. Take Neil Bissoondath, who might agree with the analysis that Canada possesses said meek national iden-tity, but whose solution seems disturbing:

> Canada is a country greatly diminished since the Second World War. The truth is, we carry little weight in the world ...[with one common national identity]...Then the rest will follow, the collective sense that we, secure in our individual selves, all share in and belong to a large, old and ongoing enterprise. From out of our gentle chaos will emerge a country unimagined, with purpose beyond survival and influence be-yond rhetoric. Only then will we – and the world – be convinced that we truly exist.[14]

Bissoondath seems to allude to the deconstruction of the Canadian military-industrial complex as a sign of why we carry "little weight in the world". Would he be more patriotic if Canada could be more hegemonic, could flex some military muscle? I think this Canadian may be lost as to what the goal of a country should be. Peace is not as sexy as war, but it is infinitely times more rational. Where has nationalism led the world? Germans pressed buttons for the Fatherland. American patriotism has sent many innocent youths to their death in Vietnam and Iraq unnecessarily. Is that what Canadians aspire to?

I think that all this talk of a *need* for a patriotic and strong national identity is the purest of fallacies. The idea that the majority of citizens in a country should have a common view of the country they live in seems to be *un*democratic. The wish or calling to such a goal seems fanatical.

The question remains.

If no national identity is required: what is Canada to be?

Is it not obvious by now?

Canada can be a 'world society': global citizens living within sovereign borders of historical convenience. Perhaps if Canadians stopped looking for what identity should unite us, they would see that in Canada we are already working together. By definition, an identity is exclusive; some people fit into the identity's periphery and some do not. It is not in Canada's best interest to be exclusive. Canada possesses a diversity of citizens in background, faith, ethnicity, and mentality: working and living together in a society. Canadians come from all parts of the globe. Canadians set an example of how the (not so) different people of the world can live together, without being coerced by a uniting goal. I think of myself as a citizen of Canada, and I also think of myself as a citizen of the world. If someone where to ask me where my allegiances lay, pressed me to say whether I was first and foremost a citizen of Canada, or of the world, I would have to ask them "Should there be a difference?" The standard of Canada's success should not be measured by whether every citizen defines 'Canadian' in the same way. What *is* paramount to ensuring that Canadians continue to work together and move in a positive direction is not to establish a national identity, but to further develop a society that represents its citizens.

2

Political Mindset:
Post Modern Democracy

"if globalization has given rise to the view that unfettered capitalism is the only course of action – what the French are aptly calling "la pensée unique" the only view that is accepted – then it seems to me that the liberals did not deserve their victory over the socialists in 1989, and that, in the more or less short term, Liberalism could become rigid and then paralyzed, like Communism before it. This is the fate of any system that sees itself as a scientific truth"[15]
> – Pierre Pettigrew in "The New Politics of Confidence"

"I am more convinced than ever that a lively two party system is essential to our democracy."[16]
> – Stockwell Day, addressing Harvard Law School, 2005

In Canadian politics, it seems all those in a position of power could benefit from one shared characteristic: having an open mind. An open mind means the ability to acknowledge the possibility that you could be wrong, as well as being able to interpret incorrectness as a prompt to change. I would love to hear the leaders of political parties recount how they were wrong at points in recent history. It would make them more: believable, human, and even more trustworthy. Being wrong can come in a variety of degrees and circumstance. It could be that a person is merely misinformed; they misheard, or misinterpreted information. If a Canadian politician is talking about hockey and says "puck", another politician might hear another word, which is not commonly linked to things as wonderful as a discussion of hockey. Another common cause of being wrong is not fully reviewing all the facts and arguments at hand in a debatable situation. This seems to happen a lot in politics. Understandably, everyone is not expected to know everything about anything. It is easier to be uninformed. However, this does not mean a politician should not be accountable when they overstep the bounds of their knowledge. If someone claims that there is a projected fiscal crises coming in a retirement pension program, and there is not, that person should be made aware of the reality. Similarly, any government or politician that currently enjoys power should be allowed to change stance on an issue, particularly when new information is made available. However, there seems to be a more deeply rooted problem that faces politicians and citizens alike, and that is the pitfall of imbibing only satisfactory information. Let us hypothesize about the day of MP Jimmy.

MP Jimmy starts his day at his office in the House of Commons. There, he talks to a man on the phone and hears from him that such and such a government program is going well for a multitude of reasons. That information is carried to the storage section of his brain, and is retrieved during question period, as a retort to an opposing MP who claims there is information proving the program is faring poorly. The conversation usually goes like this:

Opposing MP: Mr Speaker, it has come to the attention of the country that program [such and such] is very ineffective, according to a recent [so and so] report. There are no positive results, and the program is fiscally unbalanced. Can the government admit that it has mismanaged another portfolio and that this program should be scrapped? [The last sentence can be substituted for any other menacing, made for TV, question period question]. (*Opposition applauds*)

MP Jimmy (who is responsible for the file of program [such and such]: Mr Speaker, the goal of program [such and such] is to provide Canadians with [positive adjectives, i.e. security, or health] and the government feels, unlike the opposition, that [said adjective(s)] is important to Canadians and is in the best interest of Canadians, and the government will continue to do what is best for Canadians. (*Government MPs applaud*)

What is interesting is that the day before, when the same criticizing report on the program was read by MP Jimmy, the information was not zipped quickly to his brain for useful storage. It was either quickly dismissed, or it was seen as an impediment to his objectives, an attack to be repelled, not a reason to review his stance or mandate. There is a term for this: 'selective hearing'.

The effective politician, or policy maker, takes *all* information into account, and is accountable to them self: confident their position is not carved in stone. Today, politicians are deficient in doing what is necessary or right; but always carry out what their aspirations or ideology expects. What if the Bloq Quebecois, part of whose mandate is to 'look out for the best interests of Quebeckers' became aware that only 15% of Quebeckers still thought that the pursuit of separation was a necessary one; that the other 85% thought that a party representing the regional interests of Quebec at the federal level was a good idea, but did not want Quebec to separate? How quickly could the party adapt their mandate to no longer vigorously pursue 'independence for Quebec'? Would the people who run under the Bloq Quebecois continue to 'look out for the best interests of Quebeckers' and maintain their support? Or would they stoically keep separatism as part of their platform and see their popularity whittle relative to the newfound disparity in its support? What if the federal Liberal party became aware that the great majority of corporate citizens wanted a healthy environment? That mainstream corporate ideology in Canada had transformed into a willingness to ensure a healthy environment as long as commitments were equal so that one company or sector could not competitively undercut another. Corporations are just made up of people, and perhaps informed people will care about the general condition of their environment. If the Liberal party, so conscious not to impinge on a free market devoid of serious environmental regulations, heard of this, would they be able to change their party stance? Would they be able to institute environmentally friendly regulations that did not disrupt the corporate playing field?

How underrated a characteristic: the ability to admit you were wrong. No one is going to be correct all the time, and in politics it seems some would rather die maintaining they were right, than make the best conceding they were wrong. Today political parties are constantly trying to tear each other down while maintaining a 'perfect' record to the public audience. In sound bite news, who has time to admit they made a mistake, misjudged an issue, and are reworking their approach to it? This seems less than optimal. Let us take the Liberal government while Paul Martin was finance minister. He erased the deficit, and churned out plenty of surpluses; he also put a dent in the national debt, cut corporate and individual taxes to stimulate economic growth with key timing to ride the wave of the 90s boom. However, many things resulted from this economic growth. The gap between the rich and the poor increased, and certain domestic programs languished. It also seems that understated surpluses (and accountability) allowed for a lack of fiscal disciple in programs like the gun registry, and when coupled with regulatory loop holes, the existence of slush funds that can be highlighted by the sponsorship scandal. What did Paul Martin do since the time this became publicly known? Did he immediately apologize to Canadian citizens? Did he say something like:

> As you know, we accomplished a great deal of things while I was finance minister, and my predecessor Jean Chrétien was Prime Minister. We reduced the debt, we got Canada back in a position to be eco-

nomically competitive in the world market, and we handed in plenty of surpluses. However, in our surge we seemed to have let some things slip through the cracks and we need to learn from these lessons of undisciplined fiscal spending. I acknowledge that the boom of the 90s, though largely deemed a positive, was not a great thing for every single Canadian. I will make sure we do not forget those lessons, and try to evolve our strategy of economic development to make sure that continued economic growth is good for all Canadians, that government books are accountable, that we erase corruption.

From the time the Auditor General publicly unmasked the sponsorship scandal on May 8th, 2002, to when Martin made an apology in his nationally televised address on April 21st, 2005 the closest thing he said to that was "I could have shovelled all of this [the sponsorship scandal] under the carpet"[17] in the June 2004 national debate. Why did it take nearly three years for Paul Martin to publicly apologize? One needs only to look at the level of public pressure that was placed on the federal Liberals immediately preceding Martin's address to the country, to see why it was so long coming. It took the risk of the Liberals losing power in government to force Martin to do what he should have done right away. Of course most Conservatives will tell you that he took so long and postured so much because of his *personal* involvement in the sponsorship scandal.

But this is the point. Conservatives will say anything that indicts the Liberals, especially the Liberal leader, Paul Martin in this case, in a negative way. Even when they clearly have no knowledge of the facts. Just the same Liberals will raise scare flags, when for example the Conservatives made a large push in the July 2004 federal election. When the Conservatives started to close in the polls, Liberals tried to scare Canadians with commercials that said, "Stephen Harper would have sent troops to Iraq. Stephen Harper would build aircraft carriers and tanks for the Canadian armed forces. Stephen Harper will take away a women's right to choose." *Even if all these things were true*[18], it is not the place of the Liberal campaign strategists to tell the Canadian public what Stephen Harper would do. The public should not have to trust what the other guy is saying. Perhaps the public would be better suited if they got their information about each political party from a source that did not have a vested interest in falsely representing a party. The media often fails in this respect. Television news has displayed a propensity to only show the commentaries of the MP Jimmies of the world. Or is it that every politician the television interviewers can find has been trained by an MP Jimmy?

Going negative occurs when the other guy starts telling voters about a party's policies. Once a campaign goes negative, (or starts negative as was the case in the 2004 American Presidential Campaign), informed discussion and factual debate is obstructed, relative to the degree of negativity. The 2004 American Presidential Campaign is a perfect example, as there was inconsequential informed national debate, whether in the media, or across groups of people. Those who were anti-war/Bush before the campaign did not change anyone's opinions with facts, or arguments, and those who voted Bush last time were overwhelmingly devout in re-electing him. Those who were pro-Bush before the campaign were so caught up in the negativity that they became defensive. Defensiveness in this case, resulted in stubbornness and led to immobility in one's vote for president.

Canadian politics seems to have shown flashes of this type of behaviour, though thankfully, Canadian voters en masse do not seem to have labelled themselves as Liberals, Conservatives, etc. I do not think that Canadian desire to follow the trend of the majority in the United States, which is to pick a side, stick with it (be loyal), and do everything you can to undermine the other side. There is a most fundamental difference between the mentalities of "I am a Republican." and "I voted for the Republican Party." A person who defines themselves as "a Republican" such as the majority of the people who voted for President Bush or Reagan, has a predetermined instinct to defend that label, even if it is self defined. If the Republican party, in a broad sense, does or condones something bad, (like invading another country), you could say, "well I sure made a mistake voting for them" or you could say "well they must be right!" You could reinforce some illogical arguments – arguments you might have not otherwise believed had you no interest in being right – to convince yourself in some way what they did or are doing, is correct. If you say to yourself, "I am a Republican." do you think you would be more likely to go with "well I sure made a mistake voting them in" or "well they must be right, I voted for them, he says such and such on TV, you don't vote against a war time President, we should support the President, and we need to be patriotic." The first response obviously characterizes someone with an open mind, someone who has the ability to consider that they could be wrong. The second implies someone whose label of themselves is under a type of attack, whether self imposed, facilitated by the media, the people and discussions around them, family heritage, whatever the case may be. When that label of self is under scrutiny, people have a tendency to become defensive, searching everywhere to find an argument that can bail themselves out, and defend the label. If someone left the American 2000 Presidential election with the feeling "I voted for the Republican Party." as opposed to "I am a Republican." do you think they would have been more or less likely to consider changing their mind to vote for John Kerry in 2004? Let us apply this idea to Canadian politics. If someone says "Well I am conservative." what does that mean? Does it mean that they favour fiscal diligence and a minimization of frivolous spending? Or does it mean that they do not support, for whatever reason, same sex marriage, the legalization of marijuana, or a far-reaching welfare program? Does it mean they wouldn't mind privatizing health care? It is hard to say from the statement what an individual would think about these issues, and their opinion on each may vary in extremity and moderation. The most likely conclusion one can make though, is that they will vote for the Conservative party in an election. This is problematic. It reduces the chances a voter will hold the party they voted for accountable. It increases the chances they will memorize the negative things they hear about opposing parties, and forget the negative things they hear about their own party. It increases the chances that – when directly confronted with evidence that their party did something or supports something they would otherwise consider wrong – they will become defensive, stubborn, in other words not open minded. Of course, this dynamic is not found solely in the Conservative party, in fact, I saw many smiling young people say "I am a Liberal" at the Liberal Policy Convention March 2005, and I am sure that there are some young people attending York University working on Jack Layton's election campaigns who would say "I am a New Democrat."

Avoiding certain labelling as much as possible, namely in the political arena, would seem to lead to open discussions, whether within an individual's mind, or amongst different groups of people. If you look at other forms of social, political, and especially religious labelling, they are inherently negative. Extreme examples are easy to come by. Historian Howard Zinn puts this idea in context:

> In the history of the human race, we have often seen certain words used to stop thinking, to end rational discourse, to arouse hatred, words which are murderous. The word Jew and nigger have led to mass murder and lynching, and enslavement. The words Catholic, Protestant, and Moslem have been used to inflame religious wars. The word Communist in this country [America] has been such a word.[19]

To avoid a problem of similar influences – albeit of lesser magnitude – when applying extreme examples, the lessons do not change. In a political context an open person would try to avoid labelling themselves as following or being of a specific party, even in the case where they are working for, or running for a specific party. From that would follow interpreting each individual issue based on its merits. If this does not occur, a citizen would be predisposed to set their party's stance on an issue by default perhaps without thinking.

Recently while in Texas I befriended a young American who considered herself "a Republican". When I raised my concerns about the choice between only two parties she explained, "Well, when you think about it, there is really only two ways to look at an issue." This may be sustainable if there was only one issue at hand. If the issue was same sex marriage, then all the citizens who were against it would vote for the party opposing it, and all the citizens for it would vote for the party advocating it. But what if there was more than one issue? What if there were only two parties, and there were two issues: abortion and same sex marriage. If you took the 'pro-life' view and were against same sex marriage, it might be clear who to vote for, just as it might be clear if you took the 'pro-choice' view and were for same sex marriage. But what if you were against same sex marriage but 'pro-choice', or for same sex marriage, but 'pro-life'? If there were only two parties with opposing views on everything you would have to place each issue on a scale of your convictions and weigh their opposing magnitudes. After that, in choosing to vote, you would be compromising your belief on an issue by voting for a party; less than an ideal system. As modern Canadian voters face a multitude of issues that are complex with choices that are not binary, this is a hypothetical.

Canada's southern neighbour however, has only two parties available to realistically choose from. Realistically, not only because there is a no legitimate third party. Realistically, because the binary choice is a hypothetical, the two dominant parties have had the same stance on same sex marriage and abortion, as well as the vast majority of other issues. The difficulties Ralph Nader had getting his name on the ballot in some US states display the problem of a lack of choice. Not only could a citizen of the United States not procure a spot on the ballot, but the Democratic Party tried all legal means to keep him off. This effort was a result of the 2000 election where, according to the pundits, Ralph Nader 'cost Al Gore the election'. The thinking being that the majority of voters who voted for Ralph Nader would have, if he were not on the ballot, voted for Al Gore. This motivated the Democratic Party's attempts to keep Nader off of the Presidential ballot in 2004. Who Ralph Nader is and what he stands for is not relevant to the point: if a citizen of a country cannot run for an office of which they are a constituent, then the situation is undemocratic regardless of whom that citizen is. This is an example of the problem of consolidating power, reducing variety and choice in the political system. In this case, the two parties are not only wrestling each other for standing, but also making sure that no third power emerges.

The obvious lack of choice found in the two party system of the United States raises concerns about the Conservative merger in Canada. Many views in both the Progressive Conservative and Reform/Alliance ranks have been lost in this merger, in an effort to gain power. Stephen Harper, formerly a self labelled 'libertarian' when it came to social issues is one example of views being left in the shuffle. He has spoken out against same sex marriage as head of the Conservative party, when not long before, he roughly thought that the government had no place in the bedrooms of citizens. Perhaps his belief in social libertarianism had to be weighed against fiscal conservatism or his desire to present a Conservative challenge to the Liberal party.

How many parties do Canadians have to choose from? The 2004 election yielded only four parties with seats in the House of Commons. There was also one elected independent. The biggest difference in the Canadian political landscape between the 2000 election and the 2004 election was the consolidation in the Conservative ranks. The Canadian Alliance, formerly the Reform Party, and the Progressive Conservative Party consolidated their power by merging, in order to make a run at the Liberal Party. The problem with this is multifaceted. Firstly, it narrows the choices that people have. There was, believe it or not, a difference between these Canadian 'right-wing' parties before they merged together. The motivation for the merger was 'to become a competitive alternative to the Liberal party', who had dominated the federal landscape for more than a decade.

So let me get this straight: it is more important to try and gain power at the compromise of a party's ideas, than maintain a representation of differing views. Canadians should be wary of where this leads. The inertia of such a trend stops with the formation of a two party system similar to that of the United States. From a Canadian perspective, there does not seem to be a lot of difference between the Democrats and Republicans. Both parties, from 2000-2004, supported the death penalty, supported the wars in Afghanistan and Iraq both monetarily and ideologically, did not support public health care, did not support same sex marriage, supported tax cuts for the rich and big business, supported free trade market agreements while simultaneously supporting protectionist policies for the American beef, as well as the majority of domestic industry. Neither party said much about the health of the environment, or reducing poverty at home or abroad. The primary difference between the Democratic and Republican parties is that each thinks they should be in power instead of the other. Labelling dominates, and can be exemplified in the

2004 election. The American media is of course complacent in this low level of exchange; it involves less work delving for substance. The Democratic Party tried to label George Bush as a warmonger, a reckless spender, a 'divider', a friend to the rich and an enemy to the poor. The Republican Party on the other hand, branded John Kerry as a liberal, a flip-flopper, an elitist, soft on terrorism, and unrealistic on the war in Iraq. In hindsight it seems that the Republican public relations team won the negative labelling campaign, and hence their party gained power. It seems to me that the reshaping of the Canadian 'right' from the separate entities of the Reform Party and the Progressive Conservative Party, to the Progressive Conservative Party and the Canadian Alliance, and to the final conglomeration that is the Conservative Party, bastions itself to less diversity of views, more consolidation of power, and more compromise in the opinions of the party's supporters and members. Now, I sympathize with citizens who feel that they need to band together on the 'right', to oppose the Liberal party's dominance. They feel that if the same party gets elected every time, in this case the Liberal party, there is no democracy. It is unfortunate that they feel the need to compromise their individual ideas in order for the system to become more democratic. An electoral system that does not inhibit parties from remaining distinct in their views, yet does not allow for the monopolization of power, is clearly an answer.

Fair Elections[20]

Let us hypothesize. First, imagine that you are the Prime Minister of Canada. Second, imagine that you know, in your heart of hearts, that you are the best person for the job, and that you can do the job better than anyone else. Also, let us say that you got elected by the people under the current election format. Finally, let us say that you have become aware that the current electoral system has made it more likely that you will be re-elected in the future. Bearing in mind that you are the best person for the job, would you be predisposed to reforming the electoral system so that it is fair, or would you focus on other priorities like health care, foreign policy, equalization, getting yourself re-elected, etc? If you were not the Prime Minister, would you trust them to take initiative to reform an unfair electoral system? Professor Henry Milner had this to say in his editor's introduction to the book "Steps towards making every vote count: Electoral Reform in Canada and its Provinces":

> Despite urging from prestigious bodies like the Law Commission of Canada and new prime minister Paul Martin's commitment to reducing the democratic deficit, the ruling Liberals refuse to consider changing

a system from which they benefit greatly to one in which they would probably have to share power.[21]

There are two houses in Canada's federal government. The Senate is the 'upper' house whose members are appointed by the Prime Minister. Citizens become eligible for the Senate when they are 30, and if appointed, must retire by age 75. The House of Commons – the 'lower' house – is comprised of members elected based on what is called a First Past the Post system (FPTP). The system is based on a set of geographical divisions, each roughly equal in population. For example, there were 308 divisions or ridings, in the 2004 federal election. Each riding represents a seat in the House of Commons: the person elected from the riding represents its inhabitant, or constituents. A benefit of this system is every person from every part of Canada is represented in Parliament. However, as implied before, this system over-rewards the most popular party with seats that are not a representation of their popularity. For example, if there are 10 seats/ridings, and the Liberal party receives 60% of the vote, with the Conservative party receiving 40% of the vote, then you would expect there to be 6 Liberal seats, and 4 Conservative seats. There is no guarantee this will be the case in the current system. If the Liberals received 60% of the vote, *in each riding*, and the Conservatives received 40% of the vote in each riding, then the Liberals would win every riding, and hence have all 10 seats in the legislature. Outlandish examples of this flaw at work can be found both in provincial and federal results that utilise the FPTP system. For example, in the 2004 federal election the Bloq Quebecois received 54 seats in parliament with significantly fewer votes than the NDP who received 19, (1.67 million votes compared with 2.12 million). In 1987, Frank McKenna's Liberal Party was elected as the government for New Brunswick. They received 60% of the popular vote, and 100% of the seats. That is not just undemocratic, it is nonsensical.

This is an issue that affects all Canadians and has presented some interesting solutions. One idea is that a form of proportional representation (PR) should elect the House of Commons. PR suggests that the number of seats a party earns to represent the party's ideas in the House of Commons is in equal proportion to the percentage of votes they receive. In that system, given the previous example, there would be 6 seats for the Liberals and 4 seats for the Conservatives regardless of where the votes where cast. Sounds fair? The idea is not without problems. It is obvious that Canada is a large country, with a variety of regional interests. Let us use the regional example of the elected independent representative in the 2004 election (the late Chuck Cadman,

Surrey North). He received only 14,765 votes, or 0.12 percent of the national vote. To gain a seat in the House of Commons (under straight proportional representation) he would have had to receive 1/308th% or 0.32% of the total vote (over 43000 votes). However, he clearly was the best representative of his riding's desires because he received the most votes from that riding. It has been argued that pure proportional representation could decay two things in federal politics: regional interests and direct representation. From that statement perhaps some would point to Quebec as the problem, being considered the most politically divergent region in Canada. However, the current system is not just enhancing Quebec's regionalism. The fishing industry in Newfoundland is much different than that in British Columbia, and therefore requires different representation. The beef industry in Alberta is different than the cherry and apple industry in southern Ontario. From the provinces' perspective, they were technically once autonomous and voluntarily joined into the federation that is Canada: but they did not give up their own provincial sovereignty when they did. Therefore having MPs that represent geographic areas within their provinces – not MPs who just holistically represent Canadians – is in their interest. On the side of direct representation, citizens have to have someone who is local to hold accountable and make them aware of local issues. What Canadians do not want to lose with electoral reform is the right of constituents to present petitions to their local MP who is then obliged to read it in the House of Commons. Due to the regional differences in Canada: urban versus suburban versus rural or those found in industry, lifestyle, and environment as well as provincial and regional mentalities: a fair electoral system must represent these different views. What is a democracy if different interests cannot be represented and different views expressed?

One benefit of a proportional representation system would be that current fringe parties, *with widespread support*, as opposed to regional support (like the Bloq Quebecois) would be granted a voice. The Green party is an example. In the 2004 federal election, the Green party received 4.3% of the popular vote or 582,247 votes (see Figure 2.3). Yet, they received no seats in the House of Commons. **4.3% of 308 is 13**. If those five hundred and eighty-two thousand, two hundred and forty-seven Canadians had stayed home and not voted, the end result in the House of Commons would have been exactly the same. That is not the mark of a democratic system. The problem for the Green party is that it enjoys wide spread support that is not concentrated enough in a single riding to gain them a seat under the current system. Our previously mentioned independent MP only received 14,765 votes, more than half a million less than the Green party, and he got into the House! On the other side of the spectrum, it has been argued that the Progressive Conservatives would still be a federal party today if the electoral system had been proportional[22]. Their seat totals would have been remarkably higher under PR in the last three federal elections they ran in, 1993, 1997, and 2000 respectively. Highlighting this idea is the 1993 federal election where the post-Mulroney PCs collapsed, receiving 16.04% of the popular vote, and a paltry 2 seats. Had the system been proportional, 16.04% of the 301 seats in the House at the time would have translated into 48 seats. The PCs never could recover after the collapse of 1993, especially with the emergence of the reform party, who coincidently won 52 seats in that 1993 election, without a huge advantage over the PCs in the popular vote (18.69%).

This democratic disparity is not limited to the Progressive Conservatives or Green Party of Canada, parties who were doomed and are limited respectively by the even spread of their popularity. Superficial regional divisions are also created in the vote to seat conversions of the most powerful parties. For example in the 2000 federal election, the Liberals won 100 of the 103 (97.1%) seats in Ontario, with only 51.5% of the popular vote. Conversely, the Canadian Alliance won but two (1.9%) seats in Ontario, despite having 23.6% of the Ontario vote. In Alberta, the contrast was similar but reversed. The Liberals came away with only 2 of 26 (7.7%) seats, while managing 20.9% of the popular vote. The Alliance won 88.5% of the seats (23) with 58.9% of the popular vote (the PCs taking the remaining seat with 13.5%). From these trends we can see that the First Past the Post system is *enhancing* regional differences, making them more pronounced and powerful than they actually are. It has therefore been argued that the adoption of a more representative voting system could create more federal unity, or to be more precise: it would correctly represent the actual level of unity that currently exists.

There is another characteristic of the current electoral system that creates an undemocratic situation. With the system of ridings, if a party cannot field a candidate in a specific riding, then constituents of that riding cannot vote for the party. For example, the Bloq Quebecois only fields candidates in Quebec, but if people who live in a riding outside of Quebec wanted to vote for the Bloq, they would have no one to vote for representing their views. Similarly, fringe parties have trouble fielding candidates in all the ridings, (Figure 2.1), hence denying them votes from people who would otherwise support them, but are not in a riding where one of their candidates lives. The flaws in representation through ridings show that FPTP is not a completely democratic system, wasting votes, but at the same time proportional representation (PR) has drawbacks as well. To achieve a more democratic system, a compromise between the two must be reached.

Figure 2.1: Fringe Party Candidates 2004 (out of a possible 308) [23]

Party	Leader	National Candidates
Green Party	Jim Harris	308
Marxist-Leninist Party	Sandra L. Smith	76
Marijuana Party	Marc-Boris St-Maurice	71
Christian Heritage Party	Ron Gray	62
Canadian Action Party	Connie Fogal	44
Communist Party	Miguel Figueroa	35
Progressive Canadian Party	Ernie Schreiber	16
Libertarian Party	Jean-Serge Brisson	8

A mixed member plurality system (MMP) is an electoral system that incorporates direct representation through ridings, and all the associated benefits, with seat totals that mirror the popular vote percentage. Under a MMP system, a percentage of Parliament's seats (50%)[24] would be elected according to ridings, the way they are now. The remaining 50% would be bestowed in a manner that left the final seat percentages in proportion to the number of votes that each party received. When someone went to their local poll, they would cast two votes[25]. Their first vote would be for the candidate in their riding they wished to represent them. The second vote would be for the party they support federally. The process of representing a riding would be the same: the candidate who received the most votes from local constituents would hold a seat in the House of Commons with the riding name associated to their seat. Constituents would still have a local representative with whom to file grievances, petitions and concerns. After riding seats are determined, the popular vote is tallied from the party votes. The percentage of the popular vote that each party receives reflects the final number of seats they receive: the second 50% of the seats are filled by candidates from lists in order to ensure proportionality. The Members of Parliament who were elected by the popular vote would be selected from an ordered list of candidates[26] that would be publicly submitted by each party prior to the election. The amalgamation of these two methods of obtaining votes would make the final House. The previous example where the Liberals received 60% of the vote *in each riding* while the Conservatives received 40% of the vote in each riding would yield a different result under MMP. This time, instead of 10 riding based seats, there would be 5 proportional list seats and 5 riding seats. The Liberals would again win every riding seat, because they would have the most votes in those ridings. The Conservatives received 40% of the popular vote, and hence they would receive 4 list seats because 40% (their popular vote received) of 10 (total seats available) is 4. The Liberals would receive 1 list seats, leaving them with 60% of the 10 total seats. The concept in these two fictional scenarios (FPTP vs. MMP) is summarized below.

	Liberal	Conservative
First Past the Post Seats	10	0
Democratic disparity (Percentage difference in seats to votes)	+40%	-40%
MMP Seats, ridings	5	0
MMP Seats, list	1	4
MMP Seats, final	6	4
Democratic disparity	0	0

In addition to providing a better framework for Canadian democracy, a MMP system, or a form of proportional representation in general, may increase voter turnout. According to a 2003 elections Canada study: "Voter turnout is 5 or 6 percentage points higher in countries in which the voting system is proportional or mixed compensatory."[27] Given the egregious and record-low 60.9% national voter turnout in 2004, this characteristic would be a significant upside. Another important benefit of a proportional representation system would be that it may encourage a greater diversity in members of parliament, meaning women and First Nations for example, would be represented more accurately to what their demographic prominence would suggest. The reason for this is the method by which parties' field their proportional candidates: an ordered list. The list itself would be published publicly when the campaign began. If the Conservatives were expecting to win about 50 proportional seats and the first 45 candidates on their list were all white affluent male lawyers: they might garner fewer votes because of a public backlash that they would not see if their list was demographically representative of Canada. While an ordered list does not mandate a strong, demographically representative submission where women have equal standing on the list to men, by requiring it to be publicly published at the start of a campaign, it would encourage such an approach.

There are technical things holding back a MMP (or similar) system from being implemented. The first is the number of seats in the House of Commons. There are currently 308 seats each represented by a riding. If a MMP system were to be set in place – with a 50/50 list seat to riding seat ratio – while not compromising current ridings, then 616 seats would be needed. That is a lot of politicians. However, riding size varies a lot, from 26 745 and 27 864 in the ridings of Nunavut and Labrador respectively, to 123 877, 124 572, and 119 830 in the ridings of Peace River Alberta, West Vancouver-Sunshine Coast, and Hamilton Mountain respectively. Over hundred thousand people get one vote in the House of Commons meanwhile less than thirty thousand people get the same vote? The entire population of Nunavut is 26 745, so it would be impossible for a larger riding to be formed without it encompassing more than one territory or province. Similarly, a condition of PEI's agreement to sign onto Confederation declares that the province must always have 4 seats in the House of Commons, regardless of the relative ratio to the population. Over time, guidelines have been developed on riding selection that is based not just on population, but a variety of constitutional and geographic factors as well. From this example arises another case for the need of regionally sovereign representation, while highlighting the need for proportionality: 30,000 citizens should not be equal to 120,000. PEI would never wish to give up its four seats in the house, because under the current riding size it would most likely have only one. Expanding some current ridings would be necessary to implement a MMP system. It would not necessarily mean that the number of ridings would shrink from 308 to 154, but might mean that they decrease to 175, making for a 350 seat house. Most importantly, a MMP system maintains regional and direct representation – while not enhancing regional divides (as the current system does) – and delivers fair party representation in parliament: results that are equal to voter support. In conjunction with this method of electoral reform, democratic deficiencies could also be assuaged and regional voices increased while still converting to a more democratic government by confronting the problem that is the Canadian Senate.

Senators are *still* unelected in Canada. Since 1867, Senators have been appointed by the Prime Minister for what was formerly a life term, now a maximum 45-year term. What is the role of the Senate? Originally the Canadian Senate mimicked the British House of Lords (which too was and remains unelected), to provide 'a sober second thought' to the bourgeois Commons in editing and vetting Bills. Strangely Australia, which also modelled its Senate after the British House of Lords, is unlike Canada and Britain in that its citizens have been voting for Senators since the country's modern inception in 1901. The Senate has to vote on any Bill passed by the House of Commons before it can be made law. However, no Bill has had difficulty getting through the Senate since 1987[28]. Furthermore, seats in the Senate are often left vacant for years, even a decade at a time. For the first 15 months of his term, Paul Martin left 16 vacant seats in the Senate out of 105. The length of time these 16 seats were left vacant highlights the lack of necessity the Senate has become. There was no impetus to fill these seats, and when Paul Martin finally appointed 9 of them 15 months after taking office, he was criticized. For a man who claims to be an advocate of senate reform it seemed like a hypocritical move. Romeo Dallaire was one of Martin's appointees, and arguably the most deserving of the office. However, this does not make the Senate itself democratic. I would wager that Romeo Dallaire would easily have been elected in Quebec if Senators were elected. I doubt he would even have had to run a campaign. On March 17th, 2005, a speech by former Ontario Premier Bob Rae made clear his thoughts on the Senate. An article had been published in the Globe and Mail a few days earlier citing him as a possible candidate for a Senate appointment. He alluded to this in his speech, joking that he 'was going to keep his cell phone on'. He then proceeded to state that the Senate was the institution in Canadian government that was the most outmoded, elitist, and in need of reform. If every politician is aware of this, why is there no change?

Currently the Senate does not only pass bills perfunctorily; there are Senate committees that research and survey issues relevant to government. Committee work is a service some would argue that is invaluable, as much of the findings collected plug directly into decisions made in Ottawa. It may be true that Senators do a great deal of fact finding work, coming to many interesting and important conclusions that assist parliamentarians in writing and rewriting bills. The Prime Minister may even refer policy to the work of Senate committees. The Senate's arguable utility does not make it democratic. Who is to say that a democratically elected Senate could not provide comparable 'expertise'? Not all of the current members of the Senate feel as if they should contribute to the well being of Canadians: what better motivation for Senators to do so than to have them up for re-election. The average Senator is currently paid over 120,000 tax dollars a year, with no motivation to look at their position as nothing but a reward: an invitation to sit on their ass and do nothing. Being a productive Senator is voluntary. In the fiscal year of 2001-2002, the operational budget of the Senate was 63.5 million dollars[29]. Opposition members and non-partisans alike often lament about how power is too centralized in the hands of the Prime Minister. Why then, is the power of appointing half of Canada's bicameral system awarded to him? If the Canadian Senate was democratic, the 63.5 million dollar a year investment might begin to be worthwhile. Currently it is a waste.

The Senate was also originally intended to be more provincially/regionally representative than the Commons. This was to be ensured by maintaining a fixed number of Senate seats per province. However over time this distribution has become incoherent with this principle.

Figure 2.2: Senate Seats by Province

Province	Senate Seats	Percent of Population[30] multiplied by 105
Ontario	24	40
Quebec	24	25
Nova Scotia	10	3
New Brunswick	10	3
British Columbia	6	14
Alberta	6	10
Saskatchewan	6	3
Manitoba	6	4
Newfoundland	6	2
Prince Edward Island	4	0
Nunavut	1	0
North West Territories	1	0
Yukon	1	0

After affirming that Senators should indeed be elected, the details of how to structure this institution democratically are complicated. Currently, the Atlantic Provinces are vastly overrepresented by population, whereas the Western Provinces of Alberta and British Columbia join Ontario in being underrepresented. What is more, if a system were set in place to create the Senate based on population, neither the territories nor PEI would have any seats at all. What form could Canada institute to allow the Senate to be democratic and fair? The United States employs a Senate system that in theory balances the regional sovereignties of each state (historically a necessity), to that of Congress's (relative) representation by population. In the Senate there are 2 seats per state regardless of population. The American Senate is also elected, which was not always true (it was previously appointed by state legislatures). A case can be made that the election of the Senate has made it more productive and relevant. Rhonda Lauret Parkinson for example, published a paper that remarked: "the switch from appointment by state legislature to direct election is a primary reason the United States Senate remains powerful"[31]. These ideas are interesting when applied to Canada's Senate.

What if Senators were elected with each province represented by 8 seats and each territory keeping their 1 seat? The remaining 22 seats could represent Canada collectively. How would these seats be elected? In electing multiple candidates to a position, preferential balloting is optimal. When citizens visit the polls, they would be presented with a list of Senate candidates from their province, as well as a list of federal candidates. Voters could rank their preferences of potential Senators from 1 to 8[32]. The candidate obtaining the most first place votes would be elected. The second preference votes would then be distributed amongst remaining candidates. The amalgam of those votes and the first place votes would yield a plurality for a second Senator. This process would continue sequentially until all 8 seats were filled. The remaining 22 seats of the Senate could be elected based on a one vote per person national system. There is no necessity to keep the Senate at 105 seats in size (though it may be easier to constitutionally), but the addition of 22 nationally associated Senators could avoid placing territories in an uncomfortable tie breaking position if a deadlock occurred along provincial lines. With just 83 seats, a bill put forth that Ontario/west voted for, and Quebec/east voted against, would create such a situation for the territories[33]. If 22 federal Senators were elected, the unlikely threat of provincial deadlock would not exist. Federal Senators would also have a functional mandate to not represent a specific province, but rather value what is best for Canadian citizens holistically.

The job description of a Senator is less suited to those who have a party affiliation, as it is those with professional skills and specialized knowledge. A member of the Senate cannot initiate most bills like an MP; their main role is to review bills before they are passed. The need for critical and technical skills in the reviewing of bills also translates well into the committee work in which Senators partake. Ontario would be better suited having a Senator who has little or no party affiliation, but has experience in the auto industry, or the electricity sector, or is a doctor. Similarly, British Columbia would stand to gain more if they were represented by an environmental activist or lawyer, the former owner of a fishing company, or a tourism lodge. A system of preferential voting would create space for more independent candidates – fewer politicians – representing the needs and desires of the province in the Senate. Romeo Dallaire is a perfect example of a man who should be an elected Senator. Are not his technical knowledge of peacekeeping, international relations and conflicts of unparalleled service in Senate committees on those subjects, as well as reviewing and critiquing bills passed on foreign policy?

There have been studies that show PR electoral systems encourage voter turnout; one is cited above. With more at stake in a PR system, people are more motivated to vote. Similarly, if the Senate was transformed from an aristocratic institution where terms of service can extend 45 years to a democratic one where terms are of similar length to members of parliament, citizens would have more motivation to be involved in the political process. If society strips power away from people, it is less likely they will exercise what little power they have left. In the 2004 federal election, the voter turnout for Newfoundland and Labrador was 49.3%, the lowest of any province. Do you think that the people of Newfoundland and Labrador would be more or less motivated to cast a ballot if: they got to vote for who they wanted their local MP to be – knowing that even if that person did not get elected – their vote would still go to the party they supported federally, and they got to vote for who they thought should represent their province in the Senate? Do you think they would be more or less motivated to vote if they saw 2 similar parties on the ballot or 10 diverse ones? If votes had more power, and people who chose to vote were less likely to be disenfranchised by the electoral system, do you think citizens would be more or less likely to vote?

What would have taken place in past federal elections if Canada had utilised a MMP system, as suggested above, to elect the House of Commons? Would the result plunge the country into chaos? Perhaps the tone I have used in describing electoral reform has left you with the impression that, given the chance, I would overthrow the entire system. However, changes would not be as drastic as some alarmists (including those who benefit from the current system) would rather you know.

It is a tricky order to extrapolate from any election results what would occur were the system of voting different. The main obstacle is that in the current voting system a great deal of citizens vote strategically. Figure 2.3 represents the number of the seats in the House of Commons earned in the 2004 federal election by party, and also includes the percent of votes that the party received. To contrast the popular vote percent, I have included the percent of seats that each party holds in the house and the difference between percentages, or the democratic disparity.

Figure 2.3: 2004 Federal Election results

Party	Party Leader	Seats	Popular Vote Percentage (actual votes)	Percentage of Seats in House	Democratic disparity
Liberal	Paul Martin	135	36.7 (4,951,107)	43.8	7.1
Conservative	Stephen Harper	99	29.6 (3,994,682)	32.1	2.5
Bloc Quebecois	Gilles Duceppe	54	12.4 (1,672,874)	17.5	5.1
New Democratic	Jack Layton	19	15.7 (2,116,536)	6.2	9.5
Green	Jim Harris	0	4.3 (582,247)	0	4.3
Christian Heritage	Ron Gray	0	.3 (40,283)	0	.3
Marijuana	Marc-Boris St-Maurice	0	.3 (33,590)	0	.3
Progressive Canadian	Ernie Schreiber	0	.1 (10,773)	0	.1
Marxist-Leninist	Sandra L. Smith	0	.1 (9,065)	0	.1
Canadian Action	Connie Goal	0	.1 (8,930)	0	.1
Communist	Miguel Figueroa	0	>.01 (4,568)	0	>.01
Libertarian	Jean-Serge Brisson	0	>.01 (1,964)	0	>.01
Independent	-	0	.4 (47,596)	0	.4
No Affiliation	(Chuck Cadman)	1	.1 (17, 465)	.3	.2
Total		308	100 (13,489,559)	100	

Each party has a democratic disparity attributed to it. Though these disparities may seem large, they are mollified by the fact that a minority parliament was elected. If a majority parliament was elected, which has been the case in most federal elections, the democratic disparities would be even greater (remember the example of Frank McKenna). Such a majority parliament was elected in 2000, and the hypothesized results based on a MMP system have been published by Harold J. Jansen and Alan Siaroff in the aforementioned "Steps Towards Making every Vote Count". Figure 2.4 represents the actual 2000 election results, in terms of seats, with popular vote percentage in parenthesis.

Figure 2.4: 2000 Federal Election Results[34]

	Liberal	PC	NDP	BQ	CA	Total
Newfoundland	**5** (44.9)	**2** (34.5)	(13.1)	-	(3.9)	**7**
PEI	**4** (47.0)	(38.4)	(9.0)	-	(5.0)	**4**
Nova Scotia	**4** (36.5)	**4** (29.1)	**3** (24.0)	-	(9.6)	**11**
N. B.	**6** (41.7)	**3** (30.5)	**1** (11.7)	-	(15.7)	**10**
Quebec	**36** (44.2)	**1** (5.6)	(1.8)	**38** (39.9)	(6.2)	**75**
Ontario	**100** (51.5)	(14.4)	**1** (8.3)	-	**2** (23.6)	**103**
Manitoba	**5** (32.5)	**1** (14.5)	**4** (20.9)	-	**4** (30.4)	**14**
Saskatchewan	**2** (20.7)	(4.8)	**2** (26.2)	-	**10** (47.7)	**14**
Alberta	**2** (20.9)	**1** (13.5)	(5 .4)	-	**23** (58.9)	**26**
BC	**5** (27.7)	(7.3)	**2** (11.3)	-	**27** (49.4)	**34**
Territories	**3** (45.8)	(8.6)	(26.8)	-	(17.6)	**3**
Canada	**172** (40.8)	**12** (12.2)	**13** (8.5)	**38** (10.7)	**66** (25.5)	**301**

Note that the Green Party received 0.8% of the national popular vote, the Marijuana Party received 0.5% of the National vote, and other fringe parties in 2000 received an amalgamated 0.9%.

Before the simulation is presented, may the reader note that Jansen and Siaroff's method of displaying the election result creates different ways of stating democratic disparities than I did in figure 2.3. Every cell in figure 2.4 containing a bracket indicating the percentage of the popular vote, without a seat total, indicates votes that were wasted and did not affect the overall outcome (like the case of the 580,000 votes cast for the green party in 2004). One can also use unproportional provincial results to see how many votes it takes different parties to gain one seat. In Ontario for example, the Liberals won 100 seats with 51.5% of the votes, or 1.9% of the vote per seat. Meanwhile, the Canadian Alliance won a mere 2 seats with 23.6% of the vote, a steeper hill to climb, at one seat for every 11.8% of the vote. Figure 2.4b presents the results of the simulation done by Jansen and Siaroff. The only relevant difference between the simulation and the system I outlined is that list seats are distributed in the province not federally. The advantage of this is that list MPs still have provinces they are affiliated with. The disadvantage is that it is more difficult to distribute list seats equitably within smaller provinces like

Newfoundland. More detailed descriptors about the specific attributes of the MMP system used in the model can be found in the endnotes[35]. It should be stated again that it is impossible to extrapolate hypothetical voter behaviour given a different electoral system. The purpose of this simulation is to demonstrate what would have occurred with an MMP system if every Canadian had cast their vote in a similar manner.

Figure 2.4b: Hypothetical 2000 Seats Under Mixed-Member Proportional[36]

	Lib	PC	NDP	BQ	CA	Total
Newfoundland	**3** (44.9)	**3** (34.5)	**1** (13.1)	-	(3.9)	**7**
PEI	**2** (47.0)	**2** (38.4)	(9.0)	-	(5.0)	**4**
Nova Scotia	**4** (36.5)	**3** (29.1)	**3** (24.0)	-	**1** (9.6)	**11**
N. B.	**4** (41.7)	**3** (30.5)	**1** (11.7)	-	**2** (15.7)	**10**
Quebec	**34** (44.2)	**4** (5.6)	**2** (1.8)	**30** (39.9)	**5** (6.2)	**75**
Ontario	**54** (51.5)	**15** (14.4)	**9** (8.3)	-	**25** (23.6)	**103**
Manitoba	**5** (32.5)	**2** (14.5)	**3** (20.9)	-	**4** (30.4)	**14**
Saskatchewan	**3** (20.7)	(4.8)	**4** (26.2)	-	**7** (47.7)	**14**
Alberta	**6** (20.9)	**3** (13.5)	**1** (5 .4)	-	**16** (58.9)	**26**
BC	**10** (27.7)	**3** (7.3)	**4** (11.3)	-	**17** (49.4)	**34**
Territories	**2** (45.8)	(8.6)	**1** (26.8)	-	(17.6)	**3**
Canada	**127** (40.8)	**38** (12.2)	**29** (8.5)	**30** (10.7)	**77** (25.5)	**301**

The overall distribution of seats now reflects the desires of Canadians; each party received a percentage of the total seats available close to the percentage of votes they received. Government or politics itself would not be thrown into bedlam; the order of standing in the house is similar in that both the government and official opposition remain the same. They both retain the comfortable space between them and the other parties, befitting their popularity. Regional differences remain a factor in the election, but those differences are not magnified. The parties with widespread support – like the PCs and the NDP – who received a similar number of votes to the Bloq Quebecois, a party with concentrated regional support, received a similar number of seats. The percentage of votes a party received is closely linked to the number of seats they received; yet the percentages could be even closer to true proportionality if list seats were awarded on a national level, as opposed to the provincial level, as this simulation did. The key difference between the simulation of MMP and the actual results of FPTP is that there is no more false majority, where the dominant party (Liberals in this case) receive a majority of seats without a majority of votes; instead there is a minority parliament.

Drawing from recent experience, most Canadians may think that a minority parliament is just about the worst possible outcome of an election. This characteristic however, is only true of a minority parliament elected through a First Past the Post system. With the FPTP system, a minor shift in the percentages of the popular vote can seesaw the governing party, or make the difference between minority and majority. This transforms minority parliaments in an FPTP system into 'pre-writ' campaigns, where parties are constantly jockeying for position in case the government falls, as opposed to actually doing the work of government. Paul Martin's minority government of 2004-2005 exemplifies this. However, a minority parliament in a MMP system would have a much different mindset because the votes garnered are actually proportional to the seats, making it very difficult for a party to win a *true* (as opposed to false) majority. Since slight perturbations in the polls would not make a monument difference the fall of government would not hinge on these shifts, increasing stability. If a party received 39% of the total vote in an FPTP system and was awarded a minority parliament, they might only need to jump 2 or 3% to get to a level that would transform their seat total into a majority. To the contrary, in a MMP system, the party that won the election with 39% of the vote would need an increase of at least 12 percent to get to the 51% needed to form a majority. The need for a 'pre-writ' campaign in case a trigger-happy election call was made because of slight changes in polls would be gone under a MMP system. Minority parliaments would be host to actual governing taking place. Coalition governments would eventually form, creating more dynamic, accountable, and less one dimensional policy making. For example in the simulation above, the Liberal party could form a majority coalition government, or temporary coalition with any of the four other parties. Such a coalition would not be set in stone, and could change from fiscal year, or in light of political developments. The result would be compromising dynamic policies: as opposed to the winner take all politics that emerge with undisputed majority governments.

After writing this chapter, I discovered many people believed Canada's electoral system was outmoded a long time ago. The most convincing account I have heard was in 2005 by Ed Broadbent, who outlined how fifty years ago, after much research he came to the conclusion that the FPTP system was terribly flawed for Canada and wrote in a university paper that the adoption of a form of PR would best suit Canada. He also vowed at the time to get the electoral system reformed. The fact that the opportunity for this reform has been so long in coming, may represent the general confidence that Canadians have historically shown in our political leaders. By all indications that confidence has been contemporarily shrinking.

Regional conflicts, and the reinforcement of regional identities and stereotypes, benefit only the politicians who exploit those identities. Alienation of Quebec only serves the Bloq Quebecois. Those Quebecers who in the 1990s, voted for Conservatives, essentially threw their votes away. The alienation of Atlantic Canada often serves the Liberals. The dominance of conservative parties in Alberta often leaves those Albertans who vote Liberal or New Democrat in the same situation as conservative voters in Quebec. Henry Milner describes this effect of FPTP as "hyperpolarization".

The ideas presented here on electoral and Senate reform may be unique in their details, but holistically the idea of reforming Canada's FPTP system are not original. Instead of imposing ideas – whether of British elites in 1867 or of student writers in 2005 – why not give citizens the choice of their electoral system. That is the idea behind citizen's assemblies for democratic reform. Basically, citizens representing the jurisdiction to be reformed meet in a regionally represented assembly and are educated about democratic ideas and different systems of voting and representation. If this were to happen on a federal level, there would be two randomly selected citizens (one man, one woman) at the assembly for each of the 308 ridings. After the phase of education the assembly forms a consensus about which electoral system it would like to see implemented for the most democratic results (if the system recommended is the status quo (i.e. FPTP) then the assembly disbands, its work complete). In the next election of that jurisdiction, (in our example the next federal election) an adjunct referendum is placed on the ballot for people to either vote yes or no, to accept the citizen assembly's recommendation for a new system. If the vote passes 50%+1 votes as is law of federal referendums, then the system that was recommended is put in place for the next election. As much as I think my ideas are great, would they not be that much greater if everyone voted for them to be adopted? Similarly if the First Past the Post system *really* represented what the people wanted, would not a citizen's assembly recommend it?

Citizen's assemblies are already in place, in British Columbia, Prince Edward Island, and Ontario, for the reformation of their respective provincial elections. On May 8th 2005, the citizens of British Columbia voted for the recommendation of their assembly to change the system from FPTP to a Single Transferable Vote (STV) system (another form of riding based PR). The referendum received a 57% vote in favour of adopting the new system;

however fell short of the 60% margin the government had arbitrarily set out for immediate implementation. Legally, the government of British Columbia is not obliged to follow through with the referendum's majority choice of STV (because 60% was not attained) however, 60% was a standard with no constitutional or legal precedent, as opposed to the 50%+1 usually associated with referendums in Canada (i.e. separation, conscription). As of this writing, it is in the hands of the British Columbian government whether or not to implement the electoral reform. Similarly, whoever is in power at the federal level will be hard to budge when it comes to investing in a more fair way to elect representatives: those who are in the position to change the system are the ones who are currently benefiting from its flaws.

With an electoral system that is both accountable and functional, the door for good governance is opened, yet democratic success is still not ensured. If there is disconnect between the public perception of a politician or party and the reality of their views and actions, democracy is similarly threatened. If a politician – through their own efforts or those of the news media – is perceived by the public as a steward of the environment, when the opposite is true, the electoral system's relevancy is nullified: citizens will be voting under false pretences. The need for citizens to possess accurate information is therefore imperative; yet most citizens do not have time to be journalists themselves. Citizens rely on the news media to give them accurate information.

News media companies rely on citizens as well, in that by reading their specific newspaper, watching their television broadcast, or listening to their radio show, citizens are perpetuating their existence and lining their pockets. Ideally, a company's success in income and audience would be relative to the accuracy and significance of the information they present: how well they do their jobs. Such a relationship between audience size and the veracity of news presented is not a requisite one however. In television, more prominent are factors like the level of entertainment offered, the compatibility with an individual's stereotypes, the slickness of the production, and the over-simplification of issues. The problem with audience size being linked to entertainment value is that entertainment value is often in direct conflict with providing the most accurate and informative news. In the Canadian media, a television piece on the cantankerous state of Haiti may find itself on the cutting room floor because every broadcast has to include a story on Hollywood celebrity news. Oprah Winfrey's marriage may be worth knowing of to some citizens, but it is hard to argue – with the plethora of mediums already offering such information – that it should also find its way into serious news.

As with a party system, the more views in the media represented, the better the system will function. The expansion of Conrad Black's empire, television media mergers, conglomerates owning assets in all mediums: radio, newspapers, magazines, television, and internet, are all examples of actions that risk the functionality of democracy. If every newspaper editorial views actions in the same light, if every television broadcast refuses to hold politicians accountable, and if every radio broadcaster cannot speak to topics involving their owning company when pertinent: informed public debate dies. Just as the endgame of FPTP is nearly two indistinguishable parties, perhaps the endgame of current media mergers are two competing, yet nearly indistinguishable sources of information. A society with citizens who all have open minds, and an electoral system that is the epitome of democracy will not be democratic if all the information that flows into those open minds is the same.

A limiting factor in society's progress is the system of government that it functions within. Despotism will not develop unionization. The framework that controls a system, such as a government that controls a society cannot induce moral behaviour and better standards of living, however: citizens and institutions can be limited in terms of behaviour by the system in which they behave. A system of education beginning in kindergarten and ending in doctoral research is not guaranteed to produce a Nobel Prize Physicist (though it might). However, a potential Nobel Prize Physicist may never be able to reach that potential if their system of education is limited to high school. Any electoral system cannot inherently change behaviour, and no electoral system is perfect: certain electoral systems however, can impair certain behaviour. Canadians have many obstacles in society to face both now, and in the foreseeable future. Canadians are constantly attacking these problems at the most superficial, primary or secondary levels. To be able to make true progress, one must attack the roots of these problems. What better way to catalyze progress in all areas than to implement an electoral system that is further from practical limitations in terms of democracy? If Canada's government is to be for the people, and by the people (i.e. a democracy), then it should not inhibit the voices of people by the system in which representatives are elected. If the system of government is balanced and equitable, citizens will face fewer impediments in solving problems.

3

Canadian Society:
Contemporary Change and Complacency

"In a progressive country change is constant; change is inevitable."
— Benjamin Disraeli

"We will stand, and I believe most Canadians will quietly stand with us, for these higher values, which shaped our past and which we will need in an uncertain future. In the days that follow may God guide the actions of the President of the United States and the American people; may God save the Queen, her prime minister, and all her subjects; and may God continue to bless Canada." [37]
— Stephen Harper, March 20th, 2003, in the House of Commons, on the US-led invasion of Iraq

Nearly every factor found in society changes exponentially: few are linear. When a power plant that employs 400 people opens in a small town, you can be sure that *more* than 400 jobs will be created. The 400 plant workers need doctors, teachers and babysitters for their kids, grocery and retail stores, housing, maybe a car dealership and a few gas stations. The reverse is also true. If a factory that employs 400 people is shut down, *more* than 400 livelihoods are at risk. The demand for the doctors, the teachers, and the gas station owners is expunged with the factory jobs. Actions that improve society in one respect often have multiple benefits. For example, when government properly invests in the education of the youth population in an urban area, the money spent will affect more than just the level of education. If a youth gained access to an education that would have otherwise been impossible, he or she would be more likely to subsequently find a job. Citizens who are employed – especially in a field that education afforded them – are less likely to turn to crime as a means of income. Everything in society is linked together in such a way, just as people are linked to numerous issues. Everyone is involved in either following or breaking the law, everyone cares about their health, and everyone has a vested interest in their employment opportunities. No one is interested in one thing, for example, just their education and not their health care. Each person is concerned about almost every factor in society. Hence positive or negative change in one aspect of society can catalyze similar change in others. The strength or weakness of the economy, the vigour of health care, the fitness of the environment, the population of prisons and the amount of waste collected by municipalities – these variables have parallel relationships and change in exponential terms. Awareness of the patterns of change can have a positive impact on the evolution of society. Some changes have been for the worse, some the better; some things that remain in society from the past are in need of discarding. Canadian society has changed greatly since its inception: to come to conclusions about what changes have been desirable, what should continue to change and what should remain the same, it is necessary to understand these mechanics of change.

The economic – and hence standard of living – disparities that women, First Nations, and ethnic minorities suffer from are strong examples of problems the ideas of interrelated variables and exponential change in society are fundamental to solving. The resolution of fundamental equality must take into account all factors in relieving discrimination. Education affects birth rates. Birth rates affect employment. Birth rates affect health. Employment affects poverty. Poverty affects alcoholism and drug abuse. Drug abuse affects health. 'Quality of life' factors are not the only interrelated variables in society that change exponentially. The enhancing or repealing of rights and the momentum of social dialogues follow a similar pattern. One needs only to look to McCarthyism or the Canadian women's suffrage movement to see how singular people and/or events can evoke a firestorm of state-wide dialogue. Even the spread of diseases in society follows an exponential, non linear trend. A person with a cold has no limit in their potential to spread disease. An example of an exponential effect occurs when one person gets five other people sick, with those five people spreading the virus to five more people each. Those twenty-five people each infect five people, and so forth. The power of people is exponential in effect. Rosa Parks protested segregation on busses, fuelling the firestorm that eventually consumed all segregation laws – not just on busses – but in schools, restaurants: everywhere. Changes made to society, whether in a positive or negative direction, will never be made in a linear way, and never to only one factor: every factor is interrelated and every factor's magnitude shifts exponentially. With this in mind, how can Canadians ensure that societal change is made in a direction that is desirable?

Government programs such as affirmative action and equal opportunity employment are prevalent in Canada to ensure that a percentage of minorities have the opportunity to be successful. First Nations, women, the poor, and non-'whites' are sometimes given entrance to universities and vocational opportunity because of who they are (as opposed to if they are quantitatively the 'most qualified'). This is often to the lament of males, the rich, 'whites', and most especially rich 'white' males. These programs however, are an attempt to bandage the well documented and legitimate socio-economic gaps between historically disenfranchised citizen groups and their well off counterparts. But are affirmative action and equal opportunity employment long-term solutions to the problem? What has caused these socio-economic gaps? What has caused the Canadian First Nation population to have higher rates of suicide, alcoholism, drug abuse, domestic violence, and poverty than the non-First Nation Canadian population? Why do women only make 80 cents for every dollar a man makes?

Haemophilia is a condition that certain people suffer from. If a haemophiliac is cut, their blood cannot clot as quickly as would normally be expected. Similarly, because a haemophiliac is more prone to bleeding, they suffer from a glut of internal bleeding, in joints, muscles, and soft tissue. A haemophilic can ice a bruise or stitch a wound. They can take drugs to dampen the effects of their condition, and they can receive a blood transfusion if they are in a car accident. These measures –though useful – do not solve the problem. They do not address the root causes of haemophilia; they only treat the results of the condition. Affirmative action is to the problem of inequality, like a bandage is to a haemophilic wound. It addresses the short term needs of the individual: they gain entrance to the school or are hired for the job they wanted, but it does not treat the source of the inequality.

Haemophilia is genetic. It is passed down from one generation to the next. The haemophilic is not to blame: they did nothing to deserve the condition into which they were born. Congruously the parents had no participation in their own genetic makeup, whether they suffer from haemophilia themselves or carried the recessive genes, they too were born unwittingly. Gene therapy and pharmaceutical companies are not morally compelled to invest in haemophilia research: whether it is to determine which gene causes the condition, how to prevent it, or how to assuage its effects. They do not have a legal obligation to pursue haemophilia over cancer research, or over developing products for erectile dysfunction. Some do, but are not required to nonetheless.

Today Canadians exist in a society where one can legitimately blame past generations for not doing the right thing. One can blame past Canadians for forcing First Nation's off their land, for exploiting them with alcohol, for exterminating them. One can blame them for creating the markets of the fur trade; for the overkill and obliteration of the bison. One can blame them for not granting women the right to vote. One can blame them for interning Ukrainian and Japanese Canadians during times of war, and exploiting cheap Chinese immigrant labour. I had no part in the racism of the past. I had no part in telling a nation of nomadic Bison hunters that a piece of paper said they must settle down and try to farm unfertile land. I have never treated 'blacks' as second class citizens or endorsed the idea that it should be so in law. Despite an individual's contemporary beliefs and actions, there remains residue from the past. Whether a child is born into poverty or opulence, hae-mophilia or not, is not a decision that child makes.

Christianity and Monarchy

When Canada was established as a state it was legally Christian and under the rule of a distant Monarchy. As with historical socio-economic dispari-ties between demographic groups, the modern Canadian had no clout in this founding decision. In order to counteract that lack of clout, contemporary Canadians must consider the desirability of a Christian and Monarchical state – as with the desirability of other historical issues, like socio-economic gaps or women's suffrage – as if Canada was being founded today. This mindset may be technically incorrect, but it is realistic because not only is change always possible, as Disraeli concisely framed it: "change is inevitable". The questions are where will change occur and what kind of change will it be. Traditions and historical trends are not inherently good or bad, desirable or specious: it is prudent to evaluate the merits of a tradition as opposed to en-dorsing it by default. The oppression of women's suffrage was not a tradition worth perpetuating. The argument that any country should remain entrenched in one form of dogma, whether it is a religion, an ideology, or loyalty to a crown because it has been historically is illogical.

Should the laws of Canada be based upon the tenets of Christianity? When testifying in Canadian court one must 'swear to tell the truth, the whole truth, and nothing but the truth, so help you God' on the Bible. The entire platform of today's Christian Heritage Party is based on the premise that they are the only "federal party that endorses the principles of the Preamble to the Charter of Rights and Freedoms in the Canadian Constitution"[38]. The Preamble – in its entirety – states: "Canada is founded upon principles that recognize the supremacy of God and the rule of law."[39] For context, this is the first and only place that the word God appears in either the Charter of Rights and Freedoms or the Constitution, and words such as Christ, Christianity, or Jesus never appear. The Christian Heritage Party interprets the word God in the Preamble to mean "capital 'G': the God of the Bible"[40] and at the time of the original document's writing that implication was certainly veracious. If Canada was founded today however, would that word be included?

At one time, there were only Christian schools in Canada. Roman Catholic schools dominated a predominately French speaking and Catholic Quebec. They also made up a significant portion of the schools in Manitoba, serving a large demographic of French speaking and Catholic Métis. Conversely, Protestant schools proliferated in English areas of the country. Both types of school were initially funded by the Canadian government. Historically and contemporarily, the question of what public schools should exist, what language they teach in, and what religion (if any) they should favour, has been one of divisive debate.

Questioning Christianity's influence over the Canadian state is obviously not a novel exercise. An 1890 essay by reverend William Caven (1830-1904), the first president of the Equal Rights Association (ERA), underlines some of the thoughts of those who where born into a Canada dominated by Christianity, and foreshadow certain thoughts of complacency. In explaining the views of the ERA, Caven stated: "none should be favoured, and none placed under disabilities because they are French, German, or English, or because they are Roman Catholic, Protestants, or Jews."[41] The ERA advocated the dissolution of funding of French speaking, Catholic schools in Manitoba in 1890 because the French Catholic population had shrunk from 50% of the province in 1870 to a minority of less than 10%. By 'equal', the ERA meant it was unfair Catholics receive 'privileges' that were not proportional to their population. Those 'placed under disabilities' in this case were the Protestants living in Manitoba, making up nearly 90% of the province's population, but receiving half of the government's school budget.

When it came to the question of whether the church and the state should be separate entities or work in concert, Caven was unequivocal:

> The Equal Rights movement sees no adequate remedy for the evil referred to [influence of the Church over the state] except in so defining the provinces of Church and State that the one shall be clearly discriminated from the other, that neither shall be under special temptation to seek favour from the other, and that the Church shall have to depend entirely upon its own resources in doing its own work.[42]

A critical factor in the *perceived* legitimacy of Caven's point of view is the fact that while speaking of equal rights, and the separation of powers ecclesiastic and public, he believed that: "The view here set forth is in no way allied to irreligion, and implies no failure to recognize the inestimable benefits which the Christian religion has conferred upon civil society."[43] The particular case of reverend Caven is instructive. He argued that support of a religion by the state was not a good idea, not because of the morality of the religion that was being supported – the Protestantism he believed in was at the time prevailing over Roman Catholicism in terms of popular support in Canada – but because bias towards any religion by the state was inherently a bad idea. The fury that was wrought over Ontario, Quebec, and Manitoba about the place of religion (and its historical linguistic and ethnic extensions) in society, especially in public schools can still be seen today: the Manitoba Schools Question played a large part in inflaming Quebec nationalism in the late 19th Century.

In a society with citizens who espouse a vast array of religions and no religion at all, does it make sense having the government – the representative of all citizens – endorse a singular faith? The answer was obvious when stated with only two faiths dominant in society: Catholicism and Protestantism. Yet residues of a Christian state remain in Canadian society. A recent example can be found in citizens who oppose public same sex marriage based on the idea that it is not supported in the majority of Christian faiths. If government marriage licenses are secular in nature, how is a religion's stance relevant? Churches are private institutions and have the right to declare what ceremonies are within their belief system and which are not. Mosques do not perform Methodist Baptisms. Two people can be granted a government marriage license and never partake in a religious marriage ceremony. Two people may be married in a Church, Mosque or Synagogue, and never apply for a government marriage license. The separation between church and state creates space for multiple and mutually exclusive definitions of marriage: religious (private) marriage is not analogous to government (public) marriage. The former may legally have private restrictions that disqualify certain ceremonies based on the historical morals of the faith. If the latter where to have restrictions based on gender it would qualify as discrimination as long as that law is based on the Charter of Rights and Freedoms. In this example, valid arguments for or against the government's legalization of same sex marriage, in a country that enjoys a separation between church and state, would be secular in nature.

The fact that Canada was founded as a Christian state should not be blighted from history books: acknowledging it as the dominant ideological influence in Canada's past is invaluable to understanding what Canada is today. However, if further equality and coexistence between people is desirable, maintaining the separation between government and church is preferable, regardless of the morality of a religion. Why then is the Bible still being sworn on in court? Why is the word 'God' in the Constitution? If largely ceremonial matters seem parochial to you, why are Canadian taxpayer's dollars being spent – in large amounts – to fund Catholic schools?

Should the British Monarch remain Canada's head of state, if merely in technicality? Currently Canadians are paying the salaries of ceremonial positions, the governor general and lieutenant governors, who symbolize Britain's colonial rule over Canada by acting as the British Monarch's representative in Canada, or a province, respectively. A monarch by definition is a person who is worth more to society than others, a person who rules over others. Approving this idea, however tacitly, would contradict the idea of the fundamental equality of all citizens – an idea Canada supposedly endorses. Often the reason cited for keeping the monarchy involves the notion that Canada would not want to offend contemporary Britain: that by keeping the link of monarchy, the international bond between Britain and Canada remains strong. Does not Canada have ambassadors, embassies and consulates in Britain? Would the British population, who largely view the Monarchy as outmoded, feel scorned if Canada separated itself from this vestige of imperialism? If this vestige of imperialism was divorced from the Canadian government, would British economic and foreign policy towards Canada change for the worse? A more credible argument for keeping the office of governor general (or lieutenant governors) is to settle parliamentary disputes. Does an office that is appointed by the Prime Minister to resolve parliamentary disputes have to also be the British Crown's representation in Canada? Two obligations: representing a monarch in a colony, and making a ruling on the dissolution of parliament do not seem to be necessarily linked in any practical way.

Often when the subjects of abolishing government connections to the Monarchy, disconnecting the historically Christian foundation of the Canadian legal system, and separating overtly Christian symbols and language from Canadian institutions are broached a common alarmist argument is usually stated after these conditions are established to be less than ideal. The idea being that a state with a ceremonial Monarchy is a necessary evil because of the bedlam that will ensue with its abolishment: that politician's and parliament's mindset will change to that of royalty or that the country will fall apart without a uniting, supreme ruler. Winston Churchill once described constitutional monarchy as 'the least worst' of all systems. Similar themes can be found in Christianity's influence. An example can be found in the commandment 'Thou shall not kill'. Legally a Canadian citizen can not kill anyone, and this law is congruous with Christian ideals. As with abolition of the Monarchy, using Christianity as a moral compass to base the rules and laws of society is often stated to be a necessary evil because without that base, society would have no moral compass, and therefore might deteriorate into chaos. The idea that society will deteriorate or government will fundamentally change with the abolition of the Monarchy or the complete separation of Christianity is rooted in reasoning that is eerily similar to the idea of needing a national identity: in that they all are frivolously conjured necessities that in reality cannot possibly exist. The British Monarchy's rule over and connection to Canada currently has no more than a ceremonial effect on government besides draining money from its budget; its removal would stop funds from being wasted and end Canada's acquiescence to the idea that there is a person on the earth who is above all others. The Prime Minister would still be legally contained within the House of Commons and remain the head of state: his powers would not need to be extended. There can be no power vacuum in the absence of power that was ceremonial. Christianity is no longer the dominate influence in today's legislative motions: a practical approach of trying to solve problems is. Is murder is illegal because a religion proclaims so, or is it illegal because making it so provides a disincentive for people to kill one another? A Christian influenced Canadian state, as with a Canada retaining the British Monarchy's ceremonial rule, is no longer (if it ever was) a necessary or least evil: it is a relic, a vestigial evil.

Complacency

Breaking the law is not always immoral. Should a 'black' man be punished for sitting in a restaurant with a 'white' man if it were against the law? Change towards equality and the resistance to change will always be prevalent so long as there are those who benefit from injustice and those who fear such change. When authority perpetuates injustice it may be necessary to undermine authority. Violence is never a justifiable part of change. However vandalism is a crime and it may be a crime to vandalise a "whites only" sign: but is it unjust? It is a fallacy to think of the law as a black and white guide to what an individual should or should not be able to do. Often this fallacy provides those in power an excuse to help maintain the current balance of power: the status quo. In many cases of the status quo, the law is the instigator of the injustice: such as a law refusing women the right to vote. A failure to recognize the possibility that law could be creating injustice leads to a complacency that many Canadians suffer from today.

Some Canadians believe in a broad sense that 'things are the way they should be', in terms of human rights and society's machinations and structure: that looking back into the past all the goals of equality have been reached. Citizens think of the past as filled with barbarism and injustice, and when current reflection occurs, those things that are suboptimal are overlooked. Similarly, Canadians often (correctly) perceive other countries to be harbourers of iniquity and injustice. When comparing the general state of Canada and the general state of Afghanistan for example, one could declare that they are looking into Canada's distant past. However, this type of thinking is akin to that of the 'perfection by comparison' discussed in the first chapter of this book. When individuals in society look at the past and the state of other countries, they can become complacent in their current state.

Canadians should be thankful of the progress that has been made, that society has evolved over time. Canadians should also be thankful to live in a county not plagued by greater hardships. These relatives however, do not entitle citizens to become complacent. One could argue that it would be unappreciative to those who struggled in favour of the current forms of equality to stop now. Current Canadian society can be improved. A critic might rejoinder that the world cannot be made perfect. The world is far from perfect: perfection is nowhere in sight. The definition of a perfect society or utopia is one that is variable and general. The continued push for progress and equity can be defined by present and attainable goals: it is discrete. Once a definable goal of equity or progress is reached, then the search for the next hill to climb can be made. To discount the idea of continuing to further rights and freedoms because there is no end goal in mind is self-defeating and unnecessary. Things do not have to be the way they are.

In retrospect, the battle between Catholicism and Protestantism in Canada seems to miss the larger point. Today Canadian society seeks peaceful co-existence of citizens who are Christian, Jewish, Muslim, Hindu, Agnostic, Atheist, and hundreds of other minority religions and belief systems. Will future Canadians look back and see contemporary quarrels as narrow minded: as modern Canadians see the discussion of William Caven, the ERA, the school boards, the governments, and the battle between Protestant, and Catholic influences in Ontario, Quebec, and Manitoba that dominated politics at that time? When young students catch a glimpse of the past and read in the history textbooks of segregation or certain exploitations, the concept is alien: society in the time period seems barbaric.

When Canadians of the future look back at Canadian society today, will they have the same type of view? Will they ask 'why would anyone do that?' Contemporary Canadians should *want* future Canadians to look back aghast at what society was like. Not because Canada should commit atrocities, but because Canada should strive forward from its current state. Citizens of future society should ask 'why would US law allow the death penalty?', 'how did world society let environmental destruction and disease run so rampant?', and 'why was there so much opulence in Canada and the world, and yet so much destitution?' Canadians can contribute to a future world where child poverty and world hunger is looked upon in the same way that the holocaust and segregation are looked upon today.

The fallacy that citizens have been born in a time period where society has hit the limit of revolution and upheaval, that societal progress is currently stagnant, may have a variety of causes. Youth have not lived in the past; they have not experienced the urgency of the civil rights movement, and therefore may take for granted the current state they find their world to be in. Some reinforcement of this can be attributed to the notion that the current rights and privileges that a society enjoys are self evident truths or god given. Desegregation of schools and woman's suffrage are not self evident, and were not god given. People fought for and against racism and sexism: to impose it and to abolish it. The demonizing of Protestants by Catholics and the reverse was not always present: it arose with the creation of Protestantism. Widespread and institutionalised religious persecution in Canada did not end because people became aware of the self evident. It ended because people fought for what was right. The American civil rights movement culminating in the early sixties is a perfect example of this. There was no self evident truth that 'blacks' should have the same number of votes as 'whites' or that they should be able to eat at the same restaurants, and read in the same schools. The law of the land decreed it to be so: segregation was legal and institutional. Those who fought against segregation did not always have 'correct channels' to go through with their protest. The authority endorsed segregation, and hence was the problem. There are so-called self evident truths found in the Constitution of the United States that say all men are created equal; did it take from 1775 to 1963 for those who swore by these truths to fully realize them?

Canadians rationalize a myth that the effects of power in society are fundamentally different today than in the past. That those who are in positions of authority, possessing power, would have no disputes about giving it up, if it was found to be immoral. One example of this can be found in the population's faith in the recent power acquired by pharmaceutical and genetic companies. The widespread, default belief is that these companies are out to cure the diseases and disorders from which humans suffer. The fact is altruism is not a uniform characteristic of such companies. For example, the completion of the mapping of the human genome, as well as recent innovations in stem cell research has created space for certain companies to patent genes, proteins and hormones. These are not just patents on a genetically modified seed that a company spent millions of dollars inventing. Rather, if a company were to determine which gene made a human susceptible to a certain cancer, they could patent that specific gene. Why is this allowed?[44] Biotech companies spend a lot of money on research that seeks out which gene triggers a condition. If the fruits of their labour could not be patented, other companies might simply pick up on research into a cure, without having to invest the money in determining which gene was responsible. Company A spends 10 million dollars discovering that gene x affects the root causes of colon cancer, and then company B starts spending its own money developing past that point, using company A's previous findings. However, the dangers of one company owning the rights to specific genes are also prevalent. Their ensuing research could slow the total time it would take for a cure to be found if no other company could research that strain. The company could also potentially control the market factors to create a profitable monopoly (thereby making the cure inaccessible to poor people). The monopoly of certain drugs may or may not be widespread present fact, but the conditions exist for such a possibility. This merely illustrates the possibility for such a circumstance to arise if citizens become complacent. This example arose from new developments in technology; it was not possible to envision thirty years ago. Because both residue of past oppression still exists and because new opportunities for oppression will emerge, a faithful complacency in the current state of society is an indefensible exercise.

There is another fallacy that perpetuates throughout contemporary Canadian and Western society with respect to change: a subtle form of complacency. It is that as technology evolves, so does the quality of human life and the morality of human nature. This is not true, despite what advertisements may insinuate. There is nothing self evident about more innovative, more powerful, and more efficient technology that ensures it will be used for good, or the betterment of others. Technology has the potential to assist and to harm: just as individuals do. New technology can cure diseases; it can mend wounds, build bridges, schools, and share the works of Shakespeare across the globe. Technology can build bombs and fix elections; technology can steal money, and create gas chambers. Technology has the ability to destroy the environment or allow humanity to integrate into and preserve the environment. The fallacy that technology will bring about positive change is often used as a rationalization for not acting upon current problems: apathetic citizens cite the advancement of technology as a legitimate reason to be complacent. President George W. Bush had this to say in the second Bush-Kerry debate, when asked how he would rate himself as an environmentalist: "Now, I'm going to tell you what I really think is going to happen over time is technology is going to change the way we live for the good for the environment."[45] The reason that humans have harmfully impacted the environment is because of our technology. The burning of fossil fuels, the destruction of wildlife, and the poisoning of the oceans are all a result of the use of our technology. In this case, Bush deflected the discussion of his poor environmental record in Presidential office by reminding Americans to believe in the myth that technology will save humanity from anything and everything. After questioning technology, we can also question growth. Is all economic growth positive growth? If we measure positive by an increase in the GDP, the suppression of inflation, the unemployment rate, and the strength of the Toronto Stock Exchange, then yes, all economic growth is good. The thing is: what if certain kinds of economic growth mean that the quality of life of people decreases, as in the case of people drinking more coffee. Excessive amounts of coffee are not good for anyone's health and the car's that idle endlessly in the drive through line pollute the air. And yet, with every passing year people await the new technology that will better their lives, and herald economic growth –bottom line growth – as an indicator of progress. Is a prosperous and productive gun factory more desirable than an abandoned one? Complacency is everywhere, ingrained and understated, and because Canadians in the present have not seen the injustices of the past, complacency is often a stance taken by default.

It may seem a nearly insurmountable task to 'rescue' society from the stated list of grievances and inequalities. The most empowering knowledge to affect change is to understand how it works. Factors are interrelated, no matter how seemingly distant. Factors do not move linearly, but surge as brushfires or fizzle as a naked flame in harsh wind. Generations are born into a world of novelty for their predecessors, void of the sense of urgency that affected the change to the current state. Slavery. Sexism. The Indian Act. If it is true that society's variables are moving towards egalitarianism then it is also true that the drive for justice has not yet equalled the energy spent to impose and maintain inequality. If Canada truly professes to be working towards equality and justice in domestic society (which is arguable) then Canada's projection into the rest of the world must too advocate these ideals.

4

Canada's Foreign Policy:
Aspiring Middle Power or Inspiring World Peace?

"Vietnam was a mistake: the United States thought it was fighting the Cold War, when in reality it was continuing a French colonial campaign. These conceptual errors had heavy costs. Clarity of thought is a contribution to peace." [46]

– Robert Cooper

"Canada should join the other countries that are doing this, not be the second from last, I don't think Canada will be last, Washington will help you in that regard, but I do think Canada could end up being second from last and its awful."

- Jeffery Sachs, "this" being increasing foreign aid to .7% of GDP

"You must be the change you want to see in the world."

– Mahatma Gandhi

Applying Gandhi's idea to Canadian foreign policy might yield: "Canada must be the change it wants to see in the world". I would describe a country that followed this principle as being an 'exemplary state'. A Canada25 publication invokes a similar idea as being a 'Model power' – one that sets an example for other countries in the world:

> a country whose influence is linked to its ability to innovate, experiment, and partner; a country that, by presenting itself as a model, invites the world to assess, challenge, borrow from, and contribute to, its efforts. [47]

Perhaps an example of an 'effort' in this context could be the eradication of global and domestic poverty. These new descriptions are contrasted by the term 'Middle power', which Canada was widely identified as in the period from World War One to the Korean War and for some to the present. Recall Mr. Bissoondath's quote in the first chapter: "Canada is a country greatly diminished since the Second World War. The truth is, we carry little weight in the world"[48]. Many veterans romanticize the past where as a Middle power, Canadians 'made a real difference'. However, before the question of desirability is raised: is a return to Middle power status even possible for Canada today? The norms of international interaction have changed substantially twice since the Second World War: once during the Cold War and again in the contemporary post-Cold War era. One prevailing change is that relative military strength – the very thing that defined Canada's Middle power status – is of reduced significance in sorting the global hierarchy. Conversely, because of the spread of international trade – the intertwined global market – economic strength is increasingly influential. If military strength is no longer the final authority, the arbitrator of disputes and the lone qualifier of the alpha male, one must conclude that even if Canada were to increase its military strength to the relative level achieved in World War Two, it still would not regain its (naïvely) coveted 'Middle power' status. The term is no longer relevant.

But why would Canadians wish to revisit such a state? Was the death and sacrifice of the Second World War desirable? The military industrial complex that arose in Canada during the First and Second World Wars (and had its roots in the Boer War) seemed, to the general public (excluding a sizable portion of Quebec), to be a justified *necessity*. After the fact, its memory developed into a source of pride and retarded patriotism. Howard Zinn, American Historian, and himself a World War II bombardier, touches on the American experience of WWII:

> The practical effect of declaring World War II just is not for that war,
> but for the wars that follow. And that effect has been a dangerous one,
> because of the glow of rightness that accompanied that war has been
> transferred, by false analogy and emotional carryover, to other wars.
> To put it another way, perhaps the worst consequence of World War II
> is that it kept alive the idea that war could be just.[49]

While Zinn speaks of American cultural thought, the idea of just war is prevalent among those who participated in World War II under the Canadian flag as well, and perhaps in a more perverse way. America justified war easily. First Japan aggressively attacked and therefore America was a victim. Second fascism 'had to be stopped', and without America joining the European campaign the hopes of that occurring were dubious. The reason Canada declared war, and subsequently justified it however, was very different. Canada went to war, not because it was logical, or even because 'fascism had to be stopped'. Canada went to war because of 'duty' to a colonial master: the monarchy of England. This might explain the lack of romance surrounding the war in Quebec. And as Canada's 'Middle power' wars ground to a halt, and the shell factories and shipyards where abandoned for suitable peace time industry, some relished the idea that Canada was once powerful. Some Canadians fawned over the military power of other countries…

The idea of Canada aspiring to wield greater power in an imperialist pecking order that spawned the First and Second World Wars, resulting in the deaths of 90 million people, (never mind manifested the Cold War, and such doctrines as the exploitive colonization of places like India (England) and Ethiopia (Italy), the invasion of Vietnam and Iraq (US, Britain), and an endless bombing of civilians) reminds me of a man in the ghetto aspiring to be the most powerful pimp. It is not that it would not take hard work and certain investments to achieve the rank; why rather, would one aspire to it? Why did Canada pride itself on being a 'Middle power', and why do some Canadians look back and lament of what was and could have been? We could have been bigger pimps!

Pecking orders change; Canada's ranking among states will continue to change as the features that determine rank will. International relations in a post Cold War world are increasingly defined by the developments of globalization and economic strength. If a country wishes to ignore this or any future shift, then it risks being left behind. Modern globalization has transformed the paradigm of international relations in another fundamental way for Western democracies such as Canada: foreign policy is increasingly a reflection of domestic policy. The domestic values of a country are becoming congruous to the mandate of its foreign policy[50]. The mechanisms of effective foreign policy extend from this idea: for example if a country wants to have a domestic state filled with peace, where citizens obey the rule of law, then that country's foreign policy goal's would include a world where there is peace and some rules between countries (rules that are followed). That country would then proactively advocate peace for all (not be selective), it would not engage in non peaceful activities (perhaps by invading other countries or bombing civilians), and it would not be cordial or fail to communicate its position when other countries act in a non peaceful manner (for example by invading other countries, or trading arms with countries that betray the values of peace and the rule of law). The manner in which ideas are spread and policy is implemented is, in the case of foreign relations, as important to their reception as the ideas themselves. What world does Canada want to live in? From answering this question first, the function through which ideas are presented and implemented should flow logically. And not until Canada answers definitively will there be the "clarity of thought" that Cooper alluded to: the mandate actions reflect.

Indeed a new paradigm is certainly emerging to answer that question. One that touts Canada's history as a generally peaceful, and benevolent country as characteristics requisite to putting Canada in a position to take an unprecedented step forward in the world. This paradigm of thought heeds the changes that have been wrought by a unique combination of certain world events, such as the collapse of the Soviet Union, globalization's spread of communication networks, and the emergence of non-state actors that ignore traditional state borders. It is argued that these new conditions are especially suitable to Canada: that Canada can now, instead of trying to 'not be left behind' in a Middle power world, seize upon these developments and become a new leader. The summary of "Canada in the World: Canadian Foreign Policy Review 1995" stated that:

> Canada's history as a non-colonizing power, champion of constructive multilateralism and effective international mediator, underpins an important and distinctive role among nations as they seek to build a new and better order.[51]

Though the new and better order referred to in this report is a typical Liberal party euphemism – it is not a bad idea. And while the merit of "champion of constructive multilateralism and effective international mediator" awarded to a country that bombed Kosovo in 1999, helped invade Afghanistan in 2001, and trained the oppressive police force of an illegal government in Haiti in 2004 is pretty dubious, these are events Liberal party policy statements can overlook. Reality besides, the new order alludes to goals which a more ambitious government would outline: goals that are self evident under the assumption that a global citizen should not be fundamentally different from a Canadian citizen, especially in their life's worth. A new and better order might include the end of such things as war, poverty, disease, and hunger. In contrast to the current world order in which Canada participates and some would argue benefits from: where war, poverty, disease, and hunger are commonplace.

Perhaps – as the report irrelevantly suggests – Canada is in the best position of any state to confront these things. It is irrelevant however, because regardless of ranking: any country is capable of improving the world's collective condition under the thesis of the exemplary state. To end wars, a country cannot go to war. If there is no difference between being a citizen of Canada and being a citizen of the world – that is to say: if the value of a human life is the same everywhere on earth – how can Canada justify bombing citizens of the world? To end poverty, a country cannot actively impoverish its citizens or the citizens of other countries. The exemplary state argument suggests that to create change in a system, one must present a new desired normative, for the system to emulate. For there to be no war between states for example, there must be a level of trust such that each state believes their best form of security is that trust. This dynamic is preliminarily emerging in the European Union (EU), whose peace and stability is based on concepts of trust and transparency, as opposed to deterrent force or mutually assured destruction. This trust did not form easily, perhaps a product of necessity in the post-World War II order.

The report's quotation also introduces the idea of *legitimacy* as an international resource. Canadian legitimacy can be described in this context as arising from the idea that Canada does not have a history or contemporary interest in military imperialism. While the idea of Canada possessing relative legitimacy because of a lack of military hegemony seems valid: domination can appear in a variety of forms. While military conflicts remain prevalent, sustained economic oppression on an international scale has in modernity, become more feasible.

The 1995 report also reaffirms that military strength is no longer the overriding determinant when calculating hostile interactions between states, that the most prominent strength is now economic. Thomas Friedman presents an illustrating example of this transformation in China's recent reactions to the Taiwanese independence movement. In strict military terms, China could crush Taiwan's aspirations, and the political leadership in Beijing has no aversion to using total force. Friedman argues that clearly neither military figures nor lack of political will is the reason that China has not taken an iron fist stance on Taiwan. To realize why China has not crushed Taiwanese aspirations, he says, one needs to look at the global supply chains of a company like Dell. Such global supply chains involve product parts manufactured in both China and Taiwan in an intricate and seemingly haphazard web, with shipments flowing in and out of both countries on their journey to the West. The investment of a company like Dell fuels China's surging economy. The economy's unabated growth is the key to convincing China's power brokers that the communist regime should remain in power. Taiwan's liberty in expressing its desire for independence from China can now be thus summarized. If war on the border of Taiwan breaks out: Dell stops making computers in China.

❖ ❖ ❖

Let it be stated that while Canada may or may not be in the best position to create a new and better world order, obviously Canada is in a *unique* position. Canada is considered a 'developed' and 'first-world' state, possessing a vibrant economic engine and high average quality of life. Canada belongs to such international standards as the United Nations and all the organizations its membership entails, as well as the Group of Eight (G8) nations, the North American Treaty Organization (NATO), and the World Trade Organization (WTO). Canada has by some measurements the 8th largest economy in the world, and is the biggest trading partner of the US – the world's largest economy. Canada is a post-colonial state: with a history marked by conflicts between England, France, and the United States. And while the colonial status of Canada may have ended in 1867, gradual independence from Britain had further benchmarks after both World Wars and in 1983 with the repatriation of the constitution. Often important in developing a new argument for the mandate of Canada's foreign policy is highlighting that independence as a country was achieved without a campaign of violent insurrection against British rule. Canada has not always acted peacefully post-Confederation however. As participation in the Boer War, both World Wars, and the Korean War suggest, Canada's decisions when it came to conflict during the initial post colonial era of 1867 – 1953 were predisposed, to set as a default, the policy of imperialist England.

The successful 'Canadian experiment' is a term coined in reference to the relative placidness with which the French and English cultures have co-existed since the decisive Battle on the Plains of Abraham (1759). Today, the definition has been generally expanded to the (movement towards) peaceful co-existence of all cultures prevalent in Canada –whether French, English, First Nation, third language, fifth generation or born immigrant. The emerging characteristic that Canada is a country where anyone in the world can live peacefully is not just a result of the inter-language, inter-ethnic, or inter-religious cooperative relationships that have formed but also Canada's (perceived) peaceful international stance. Canada never joined the 'nuclear club', despite the technological capability, and economic resources to do so. Canadian uranium and plutonium was used to create the American bombs of Los Alamos in 1945, and there was plenty of opportunity to join France, Britain, Russia, Israel, China, India, North Korea and Pakistan in nuclear armament during the Cold War. Yet Canada did not. More recently Canadian government in partnership with NGOs put forward the Ottawa Convention, a landmark international treaty banning anti-personal landmines. The official decision of the Canadian government to not enter either war in Vietnam or

Iraq highlight the majority opinion in Canada of warfare: it should be avoided. Similarly, Canada's high reputation as a peacekeeping force – this from a comprehensive study on peacekeeping: "Since 1945 several states have established reputations as willing and able peacekeepers, especially Canada"[52] – is in line with these decisions. All these factors, from diversity in demography, to history of conflict and past policies shape Canada's current opportunity.

A relative disposition to avoid war and a reputation for doing so places Canada in a position to succeed in the future of international relations. Yet, running America's errands in Afghanistan or Haiti threatens that success. Engaging in the bombing of Kosovo was an obvious detractor from a goal of peace. In order to succeed, passivity is futile; merely avoiding conflict is not enough. Canada must be active, pursuing courses that hinder and prevent conflict from occurring. Canada displayed with the Ottawa convention that it was capable of broad partnerships to produce positive results. Canada needs to host more summits, meeting and conferences whose goals include reaching similar agreements. Such a treaty for example, could declare non participation in the global arms trade, or a convention forbidding the use of bombing. Canada needs to work towards bringing conflicting interests together. Canada can do more to ensure long term, sustainable security. To achieve this Canada must realize that it is in its best interests that each country succeeds. Take terrorism for example.

We know that poverty and poor quality of life breeds behaviour that is extreme, including terrorist behaviour. Though terrorist leaders are often Western educated and wealthy, their disciples are usually the opposite. When youth are born in a position of destitution and orphanage they are more likely to believe the man who tells them that the West is responsible, and that the solution is to fly a plane into a building. Similarly if youth are not themselves born in such a position, but identify with a national or ethnic group facing circumstances of destitution, they are prone to be disaffected by first world surroundings. Youth who are born without choices and without the prospect of legitimate prosperity are those who terrorist recruiters prey, and thrive on; child soldiers are easier to train and brainwash. Examples range from militant children participating in the Rwandan genocide, to Jihad youths on the streets of Baghdad.

The abolishment of global poverty would heavily stymie terrorism in the first and third worlds. Both from said recruitment standpoint: those living in poverty, and those perceiving such poverty to be unjust, as well as in providing bases of operation for terrorists that are inaccessible to the rule of law. This from the Military section of Canada's 2005 Foreign policy review:

> By helping stabilize these countries [failed states], we prevent threats
> from spreading further and deny terrorist cells the haven and support
> that sustain them. In turn, this helps reduce the prospect that terrorists
> will reach our shores and threaten Canadians directly.

Once again we are presented with rhetorical euphemism: ideas that are
sound without sufficient action. Understanding terrorism in the vein seen on
September 11th 2001 (first world), or in the 100,000 child soldiers in Africa
as of 2004[53] (third world), as a non state actor that threatens Canada is understanding that the threat of terrorism is inestimably enhanced by global
poverty.

Therefore the conclusions reached when regarding global poverty –
whether one's motivation is altruistic or self interested – are indistinguishable: global poverty must end. It is by no means an unsolvable problem; if the
money put forth in every state military budget was redirected to feeding and
educating the poor, creating jobs, and wiping out the major pandemic diseases (malaria, HIV/AIDS, tuberculosis) that thrive in an environment of mal-
nourishment, the fight against global poverty might be a short one. Fallacious
is the idea that there must exist a great divide in the well-being of the world's
citizens. Global poverty did not always exist. The distinction between the first
and third world did not always exist. How then can one claim such distinction will always exist henceforth? It is not that the situation is hopeless; it is
that the commitment from rich countries, the political and economic will, is
sporadic and most often disingenuous. And yet as the policy report alludes,
it is becoming increasingly obvious that investing in stabilizing failed states
– and ending poverty – is an investment in security.

Similar to terrorism and global poverty, numerous non state actors have
emerged that threaten world peace and security. These threats have common
characteristics. For one they do not heed the division of state borders. They
also can not be combated by traditional conceptual power, such as military
strength. Poverty, global pandemic disease, refugee flows, overpopulation,
terrorism, and the degradation of the environment all fall into this category:
they pose a threat to states regardless of geographical location or military
strength. Traditional military strength in fact increases the risk of a non-state
actor like terrorism striking.

If Canada has to be the change it wants to see in the world, and the end of
global poverty is desirable, what possible course of action could Canada follow? Perhaps if a certain threshold existed such that, by percentage of budgetary money available, if every rich country in the world contributed similarly,
the tide of global poverty would wane and dissipate. Let us imagine that all

the non profit NGOs, the development social scientists, and the governmental humanitarian staff all got together and agreed that if every rich country contributed a certain percentage of their GDP (Gross Domestic Product) to fighting global poverty, over the next 25 years, certain statistics like "everyday over 30,000 children die of starvation" would change to "everyday less than 100 children die of starvation". If they came up with a number, and Canada contributed in excess, that would be leading by example.

In fact, there is a percentage level of international aid to GDP that has been cited time and again innumerable as such a benchmark, .7%. A Canadian Senate report puts the history of this figure in lucid perspective:

> In 1968, the Canadian International Development Agency (CIDA) was created to administer Canada's aid efforts. That same year, former Prime Minister Lester B. Pearson headed an international commission to examine development assistance over the past 20 years and propose policies for improvement. Published in 1969, the Commission's report, Partners in Development, called for each donor country to provide foreign aid equal to 0.7% of its Gross Domestic Product (GDP). Canada accepted this target in 1970 and has repeatedly reaffirmed its commitment. Still, in 2002-03, Canadian assistance represented only 0.28% of its GDP.[54]

Top Donors of Official Development Assistance for 2002 [55]					
Country	**Net ODA** *(in million of $US)*			**% of GDP**	**Rank**
	Bilateral	**Multilateral**	**Total**		
Denmark	1,038	603	1,604	0.96	1
Norway	1,145	552	1,696	0.89	2
Sweden	1,250	741	1,991	0.83	3
Netherlands	2,449	889	3,338	0.81	4
Luxembourg	116	31	147	0.77	5
Belgium	712	360	1,072	0.43	6
Ireland	267	131	398	0.40	7
France	3,615	1,871	5,486	0.38	8
Switzerland	765	174	939	0.32	10
United Kingdom	3,506	1,419	4,924	0.31	11
Canada	**1,503**	**503**	**2,006**	**0.28**	**12**
Germany	3,328	1,997	5,324	0.27	13-14
Portugal	186	137	323	0.27	13-14
Australia	774	215	989	0.26	15-16-17
Austria	364	156	520	0.26	15-16-17
Spain	998	714	1,712	0.26	15-16-17
Japan	6,692	2,591	9,283	0.23	18
New Zealand	92	30	122	0.22	19
Greece	107	169	276	0.21	20
Italy	1,007	1,326	2,332	0.20	21
United States	10,570	2,720	13,290	0.13	22
TOTAL	**40,734**	**17,540**	**58,274**		

The figure has hardly become irrelevant over time, as evidence by Jeffery Sach's testimony to Canadian parliament opening this chapter. As one can see, Canada is not an exemplary state in the dimension of foreign aid. Lester B. Pearson, winner of the Nobel Peace Prize for his work with the United Nations, and Prime Minister of Canada, is largely credited with developing the bottom line figure of .7%. Yet 5 countries, none of which had Mr. Pearson as a leader, have all exceeded that level of aid: Denmark, Norway, Sweden, Netherlands, and Luxemburg. That these countries have small economies, and therefore can meet the goals more easily than Canada is simply false. The Netherlands, in addition to contributing more as a percentage of GDP, also contributed more than Canada in gross. Other countries, like the United Kingdom and France, ahead of Canada in terms of percentage, also contribute substantially more in gross. In reference, 2002 was not a substantially lower year than usual; in fact in the year 2001, the percentage was an anaemic .21%.

Year to year fluctuation hampers aid's effectiveness in that it leads to unpredictability. An International Monetary Fund Report cites its recent US experience, "The U.S. exemplifies the vagaries of donors' aid budgets: the administration announced that it would ask Congress for US$1.7 billion in 2004 but it asked for US$1.3 billion. In the end, only US$1 billion was approved by Congress."[56] Canada has been equally guilty of vacillations in annual international aid. As important as the resources themselves are, to relieving global poverty, is stability in the process.

The reason that Canada has yet to reach the target of .7% seems to border on the esoteric. Jeffery Sachs, global economist, author of "The End of Poverty: Economic Possibilities for Our Time", and a chief architect of the UN Millennium Goals, a reaffirmation of Pearson's "Partners in Development", represented the United Nations at a Canadian parliamentary committee on April 6th, 2005 and made this remark with passionate incredulity:

> I cannot figure out for the life of me why Canada is not one of the countries that has made a clear commitment because this is the country where this goal started back with Lester Pearson in 1969. This is the country that championed this cause. This is a country with a fast growing economy, with a budget that can handle it, with a national leadership that is committed to these goals, and I frankly see no real obstacles – and with an opposition I might say – that has supported these goals... so it is more or less the kind of situation where I don't even understand almost as a... an act of the forces of nature what stops Canada from leading right now.

As strong a measure as raising the foreign aid to GDP ratio to .7% would be in terms of Canada tackling global poverty – the solution will not be solely a bottom line figure – especially if the money invested is not invested wisely. For many years funds have been given to resource rich, yet economically destitute countries ruled by oppressive regimes. That money has disappeared. What was intended for schools and road construction was squandered on the lavish lifestyles of a country's ruling elite, and the military that sustained its place. Nigeria and Haiti are good examples, but perhaps a universally recognized one can be found in the "Oil for Food Scandal" that took place between United Nations member states and Saddam Hussein's Iraq in the 1990s. The lesson being, funds given to corrupt governments will seldom yield desirable results. Giving international aid to Nigeria is giving your vote to the Conservatives in Quebec: in the current system under which these interactions take place there is little to no chance that the desired outcome will be achieved.

It then seems obvious to conclude that aid should be donated in methods that have a high likelihood of producing the intended results. There are plenty of countries possessing impoverished populations, such as contemporary Senegal, who would happily accept aid, and also have non corrupt, democratically elected and accountable governments. It would be prudent for Canada to directly donate only to governments that meet certain criteria like democratic accountability: collaborating with those governments further reinforces being an exemplary state. In need of disregard is the notion that donating aid should focus on states where strategic interests lie, effectiveness is crucial. Should such a shift take place, rich states might be perceived as collaborating with accountable third world governments as opposed to colluding with oppressive ones. Canada's recent foreign policy review in 2005 seemed to grip the sense in contributing aid to non corrupt governments, dubbing them "development partners"[57]. And yet Canada's actions in Haiti directly oppose all of these ideas. CIDA has been donating money to fake NGOs that are actively impoverishing the countries poor and entrenching the unelected oppressive elite.

For those suffering under oppressive regimes, globalization has yielded two methods (albeit less efficient) for modern Western governments to transmit foreign aid to a country's population while circumnavigating its government. The first being increasingly sophisticated non profit NGOs, citizen groups acting independently in charity (not for Canada's government like in Haiti). So the circumnavigation of government can be used positively or negatively: as Haiti suggests. The second method of circumnavigation is the United Nations forces that are often granted access to populations suffering under regimes and in failing states. Having a robust and fiscally healthy United Nations would facilitate aiding the citizens of oppressive governments.

A policy of only donating development aid to secure 'development partners' seems optimal. Many would see the logical coupling to this policy a mandate of actively pursuing the democratization of oppressive and unaccountable governments – thereby trying to increase the number of secure 'development partners'. Though the goal of government accountability is an important one, the methods by which states encourages this are crucial. Never would a state want to engage in actions that dissolve its achieved exemplary state legitimacy. History shows that more often than not imposed democracy backfires terribly (the notable exceptions being Japan and Germany post WWII), or more accurately, that democracy born of self determination is the most lasting kind. The effectiveness of such self determination can be seen through the actions Canada peacefully achieved democratic independence from its own colonial master. So while Canada can work with already democratic third world countries to try and create the right conditions for neighbouring populations to emulate; armed intervention into the reign of a dictator may have consequences far worse than those if the dictator remained. Populations that live under corrupt governments should not be ignored when dispensing aid, but rather the way aid is administered should be modified: with less efficient and impartial NGO groups, and UN peacekeeping forces, as opposed to through the government. Siphoning money to these groups does not ensure its good use: NGOs and the UN are inherently corruptible.

As effective as funds given to governments that use it for the good of their citizens is sharp in contrast to that given ineffectively to corrupt governments, there is a starker distinction in the finances needed to sustain unsustainable states and the finances necessary to create sustainable states. Believe it or not, the musician Bono encapsulated this idea when he said "Everyone wants the fishermen, not the fish."[58] Africa is rich in raw exportable resources, for example cotton, diamonds, sugar cane, and fish. In an ideal environment, the industries governing these resources would be nationalized by domestically owned private industry or the domestic government preparing them to be exported to the first world for a fair price, and over time lifting the standard of living and economic viability of third world African countries. However first world countries, such as the United States and European Union, heavily subsidize their own cotton farmers and fisherman, artificially driving down the prices for their stock (called export subsidies). This leaves third world countries unable to compete, driven to sell their products at break neck prices, never making a profit, and hence perpetuating their destitution.

Subsidizing domestic farmers as such is only in the self interest of America and Europe in the short term, if in their best interest at all. The low cost, mass produced corporate factory farming that produces the huge surplus in food in which the US and Europe engorges is a trivial luxury compared to the suffering Americans and Europeans experience when the side effects of the global poverty those luxuries incur come home. Refugee flows, budgetary commitments to foreign aid, the spread of HIV/AIDS, malaria, tuberculosis, and terrorism to name a few. The fact that it is in their best interest to discontinue such export subsidies is exclusive from the fact that current farming practices in both the US and Europe are unsustainable and yield such a gross surplus. Fair global trade is the genetic cure for the haemophilic condition of global poverty; foreign aid, though useful and necessary in the short term, is much closer to a bandage.

If trade was fair – that is to say if trade policies of rich countries were not engineered to keep poor countries poor – aid would be exponentially more likely to stimulate sustainable growth, as opposed to dropping in a bucket. Capitalist theory – of which Canadian, American, and European markets all subscribe to – is based on competition. If there is a monopoly in any marketplace, an absence of competition, that monopoly will abuse its power. Monopolies are anathema to functioning capitalism, and yet regarding certain global marketplaces rich states are all too quick to adopt protectionist policies, often to treat niche interests that create (practical) monopolies in the global market. Yes, there is fierce competition between US farmers and European farmers, Canadian, American, and Japanese beef farmers. That competition is on the higher plane however. There exists a lower plane upon which certain goods of the third world subsist, as a result of the policies of the perceived (and incorrectly so) self interest of the rich. Not only is the avoidance of fair trade only in short term self interest, it is only in the short term self interest of a few. American family farms face a similar situation domestically, inhabiting the lower plane to merging corporate factory farms. Perhaps with an electoral system that did not favour the ill-conceived interest of these few corporate citizens in this case; the policies residing in the American agricultural file would be different. The results of export subsidies provide an example of policy displaying how to not be an exemplary state.

The exemplary state idea can be applied to trade in a different way. Canada is apparently in a position of legitimacy because of its lack of nuclear armament. However, Canada has contributed to the nuclear armament of other countries, chiefly the United States. By exporting uranium and plutonium to the United States knowing that it was to be used to create nuclear weapons, Canada has had a direct impact on the proliferation of nuclear weapons. If Canada were to similarly export nuclear technology to India or Pakistan for example, it would guilty of a similar violation. Much of the debate over Iran's nuclear program contemporarily is whether or not it will be used to create weapons of mass destruction, or power the homes of Iranians. In 2004/2005 the Bush Administration's stance was relatively hard line; not wanting to take a chance they would rather have Iran pursue no nuclear capability of any persuasion. Russia however, took a more flexible approach, stating it would be in favour of Iran's nuclear aspirations if assured the goal solely involved benign use of nuclear power (though to qualify, it is debatable if Russia actually believes this). From a Canadian perspective, a post World War Two policy similar in idea to Russia's regarding exporting plutonium and uranium to the United States would fit with the idea of an exemplary state. If Canada was assured that the United States were to only use the raw materials procured for purposes such as power plants and scientific or medical experiments, then such exports would not leave Canada in a position of being culpable for the proliferation of weapons of mass destruction. If the United States violated this principle of trade – the moment one warhead was built – Canada would cease the export of nuclear material. Otherwise, though Canada did not directly invest in offensive nuclear strength it could be viewed as contributing to the risk of – and if it occurred, the attainment of – nuclear holocaust. If Canada values peace, and does not seek anything but the elimination of all weapons of mass destruction, then exporting raw materials for explicit use in such weapons whether to the United States, France, or Iran would be inviolable. What commodity is being exported can be as important as the price of exports in terms of the effects upon a state's security.

And yet some Canadian companies are actively *contributing* to global poverty, in some of the most impoverished places in the world, like oil rich Nigeria, where they continue to do business with corrupt militant governments. In that case, it is not just a lack of fair trade or development aid; it's a case of Canadian companies actually enhancing the chances global poverty (and the threats it entails) will remain. A system of corporate laws has made it in certain cases more profitable, for some resource companies to engage in business practices that exploit humans not bearing Canadian citizenship. This may not be the case for all Canadian business, but it does occur and it is systemic of the dogma in regulatory law in Canada: there is one bottom line and the exploitation of people in foreign countries is not the same as failing to meet basic human right standards in Canada. If Canada wants to be serious about stopping terrorism, stabilizing failed states, and preventing conflict – or in other words – saving lives and improving citizen's security, Bay Street business cannot amorally undercut humanitarian work the federal government funds by blindly pursuing their singular bottom line interest. Being an exemplary state does not merely entail contributing money from government coffers to the poor. Fitting the description of an exemplary state entails ensuring the domestic marketplace is not open to oppression. Not only are companies who do business with regimes who defy human rights making sure that money dedicated to foreign aid is ineffective, they are increasing the chances of Canadians paying taxes to house refugees when a humanitarian crisis, with all its exponential effects, occurs.

This is an example of an outdated model of law and emphasis. Akin to Canadian environmental regulations and strategy, both international and domestic, making it more likely that someone will die from smog inhalation or crops will fail. Regarding global poverty, state and non state sponsored terrorism, overpopulation, and famine, what kind of world does Canada want to live in? If a country wants a world where there is a high risk of terrorist attack and third world state failure, then market regulations should allow for business to heed nothing but their current quarter profits (short term self interest). However if a state desires a world where global poverty is not worsened by the businesses of said state, where potential terrorists do not believe said state is exploiting the third world, then market regulations would be mindful of the collective self interest of everyone, in terms of profits and survival. Simply put, if government knows what is best for everyone, Canadian owned businesses and foreign owned business operating in Canada should not be profiting with governments that abuse human rights; a logical extension of the idea that they should not abuse human rights domestically. The foreign policy issues of international aid (and interaction with third world governments), trade and business have been superficially dissected using the framework of the exemplary state, but the larger spectre still looms: the role of the military.

When American bombs killed 4 Canadians in Afghanistan, the country mourned and there was public outrage. Canada's current low tolerance for warfare, though it should not need to be, is justified. Over 60000 Canadians lost their lives in World War One, over 45000 in World War Two, and 1558 in Korea[59]. Since that period of intense war, the goal of the Canadian military has been unclear, its strategy muddled. Decisions on war and peacekeeping have been made ad hoc, based on domestic and international political factors, as opposed to a mandate or logic. Canada participated in the invasion of Afghanistan in 2001 because of reactionary domestic support and hence political justification. Canada did not join the forces invading Iraq in 2003 largely because of domestic opposition in Quebec and the political calculations of Jean Chrétien. If Canada were to have experienced deaths in Iraq on a similar scale to the American forces; the impact upon Canadian political climate would have been inestimable. From analyzing domestic political climate, one can conclude that Canadians today – the Stephen Harpers and Stockwell Days[60] excluded – do not see great value in going to war. In what manner then should Canada invest its military dollars: based on the assumption that Canada desires a peaceful world, and pursues this goal through exemplary actions?

Canada currently dispenses billions of dollars per year purchasing anachronistic technology – like submarines – that are useless to the foreign policy objective of peace. If peace was the goal, all military funding would be invested in peace promoting initiatives. Canada would not, for example, maintain ceremonial fleets of aircraft that waste millions of dollars per year. Canada would not own or operate submarines, tanks, aircraft carriers, destroyers, battleships, fighter jets, attack helicopters, or bombs. These are the weapons of war, efficaciously designed to kill people.

Canada should respect its military history; acknowledge, document and teach of the past. There are lessons to be learned from Canada's involvement in the World Wars. For example: never again. A rational country would not demean the lives of citizens lost in war by actively participating in it. Expansive military museums that maintain and restore war artefacts and vehicles, libraries and archives that extensively document the past, schools that invest in courses and textbooks on the subject of Canada's military past are all invaluable investments in future security because those who realize the full horror of Canada's military past cannot help but come to the conclusion that war is undesirable. A lack of such education leads to the patriotic romance of war: retarded and mythical.

If Canada needs an international presence: if there is a calamitous event in another country, a tenuous cease fire in a war-torn region, a mass of refugees or signs of an impending genocide, Canada should be able to deploy peacekeepers quickly and effectively. To ensure swiftness in response, peacekeepers should be able to reach their destination by air, land, and water: there is a need for helicopters, planes, ships and personnel carriers. The vehicles that transport peacekeepers should not be capable of killing people.

When Canadian peacekeepers arrive in another country, they should be a dynamic force. They should be able to provide fresh water, food and medicine to those who are in need. They should be able to defend themselves if attacked. They should be equipped with diplomatic and translation skills in order to facilitate the peace process. They should possess a cultural understanding of each community if their mission immerses them in a religious, ethnic, or cultural dispute. In order to ensure all of these abilities and characteristics, a peacekeeping force must have the full support of the Canadian government. No expense must be counterproductively spent, that is to say, no expense must be spent to undermine their efforts, in the direction of war.

If Canada had possessed such a dynamic peacekeeping force, it could have stopped the majority of the Rwandan genocide of 1994. While Romeo Dallaire and the forces of UNAMIR were left to their devices, facing an impossible task and indescribable horror, the United States hid behind policy that declared apathy in protecting the lives of people that did not fit into what was defined as in US self interest. The United Nations, with its paltry logistical support and already overstretched global peacekeepers was incapable of an effective response without the necessary support from its member states. Even if Canada had been quick to act – which it was not – it did not have the capabilities to stop catastrophe. "The failure of humanity in Rwanda" as Dallaire so accurately has named it, was not a failure or imperfection, in the structure or the fundamental *idea* of the United Nations itself, but a failure in the commitments of the powerful states in UN membership. The United Nation's ability to perform the functions the Allies had in mind with its founding after WWII has been heavily restricted. The UN has become a scapegoat for powerful countries that would rather not help those not seen (and incorrectly so) as valuable. Powerful states therefore do no adequately fund the United Nations, do not proffer peacekeepers for its missions, and block its resolutions to such a degree that makes impossible its ability to execute its mandate. Yet these states falsely lament when its missions go unfulfilled. Take the United States, who as of 2005 according to the Global Policy Forum owes an excess of 607 million dollars to the United Nations. The United States, because of its permanent standing on the UN security counsel, can veto any resolution or agreement passed in its legislature. For example, the US vetoed resolutions against the international arms trade because it is currently the world's largest producer and exporter of weapons. The United States, has scoffed at international law by refusing to participate in the International Criminal Court. Meanwhile the current Administration has insinuated that the United Nations inability to execute its mandate provides justification for the implementation of hypocritical policies – in Guantanamo Bay and Iraq most prominently.

While the federal Liberal government has issued two foreign policy reviews since Rwanda, little change has occurred. Canada has shown a similar incapacity and unwillingness to commit to peace and the lives of global citizens in Sudan. The first commitment Canada made to the region was one week to the day before a May 19th 2005 budget vote that threatened to topple the government if Independent MP, David Kilgour, a proponent of Canadian involvement in Sudan, chose to vote against the government. Even if the full political will existed, Canada does not possess the magnitude of forces necessary to stabilize the region and assist the people.

The founding mandate of the United Nations is to provide a framework within which states can achieve world peace. This framework includes the arbitration of disputes between member states, and the deployment of peacekeeping forces into spaces of conflict. Article 1(1) of the UN Charter states the purpose of the UN is "to maintain international peace and security, and to that end: to take effective collective measures for the prevention and removal of threats to the peace"[61]. The United Nations is not a state unto itself or a world government; it is a global conflict resolution mechanism. If Canada desires a peaceful world, as I am perhaps erroneously assuming it does, it cannot undermine the work of the United Nations, the mechanism by which that goal will be achieved. No institution is without problems; the UN currently suffers from endemic corruption and inefficiency. Yet it remains the only institution capable of achieving sustained peace. Despite this potential, it has yet to be given a chance to succeed. Canada needs to work to provide the UN that chance, whether it be advocating reforms to end the corruption, or challenging member states that veto resolutions. To do those things, Canada needs to be in a position where it can legitimately make such a case. Therefore, Canada needs to contribute more to the UN's institutional capacity, in terms of peacekeeping troops, logistical support, political support and budgetary commitments.

Currently, Canada spends copiously on ineffective military assets. Ceremony is the definition of waste; public assets are only valuable if they serve a purpose. For example, Canada's navy recently purchased, at a cost of 3.2 billion dollars, twenty-eight Sea King helicopters mainly for search and rescue operations. If (and this is a big if), those helicopters are durable and cost effective, patrolling Canadian waters and saving lives for a period of time that was equal or greater to their expected life span, then that will be considered an example of a worthwhile military investment.

Take however, the example of Canada purchasing four diesel engine submarines from Britain in October of 2002. The initial cost to taxpayers was 750 million dollars, which increased to 900 million dollars after the subs were refitted. The British Navy had mothballed these four submarines in

1993, nearly ten years before their purchase. The total cost to Canada is now 900 million dollars and one Canadian's life – 32 year old Lieutenant Chris Sanders, died October 5th 2005 of smoke inhalation during an electrical fire that broke out on HMCS Chicoutimi during its maiden Canadian voyage. Bill Graham, Minister of National Defence said, "HMCS CHICOUTIMI's hand over to the Canadian Forces illustrates the progress we are making in establishing a modern submarine fleet that will serve Canadians extremely well for the next 25 years." While Mr. Graham can not have been expected to predict the moribund future of the Chicoutimi, he may have simply wanted to look at the past before making such an asinine statement. Mothballed in military terms, refers to a piece of equipment that is decommissioned because it is no longer even worth running for lack of effectiveness. The fleet of four was mothballed in 1993: 9 full years before their purchase. Vice-Admiral Bruce MacLean, the commander of Canada's Navy said of the refitting process, "Despite the delays in getting all four submarines to Canada they represent a vital national asset. These vessels are cost effective and essential to the Navy and its mandate to defend Canada and its interests". These vessels are the furthest thing from cost effective. What are mothballed submarines defending Canada from? The only concrete result of the 900 million dollars spent is the death of one of Canada's own citizens. Submarines serve no purpose in international peacemaking, peacekeeping, domestic security, disaster relief or humanitarian aid and therefore should not be a part of Canada's military plan. This type of offensive military strength is an example of an irresponsible purchase made in the mould of a country trying to compete with the rest of the world in a hierarchical structure that no longer exists. What use would four shitty submarines have been in the jungle as Tutsi heads rolled?

In measuring positive impact, Canada's newly acquired submarine fleet is comparable to Canada's fleet of ceremonial aircraft, the Snowbirds. Since 1971 Canada has maintained the fleet for air shows on ceremonial anniversaries and dates of significance. Since 1971, 5 pilots have died in these displays and there have been 13 crashes. Why does the Canadian government fund an institution that takes the lives of citizens? The annual operating budget of the Snowbirds is 10 million dollars. There are claims that keeping the Snowbirds is an exercise in showing Canadian pride in war veterans. Do you see how investing money in creating an elaborate way for citizens to die is a tribute to a veteran's sacrifice? If the Canadian government desires to improve the lives of veterans, they could place the Snowbirds in museums, scrap the flying program and move the 10 million dollars a year saved into veterans' pensions.

When 'defence' spending comes home, Canada should fund a presence similar in mandate to forces abroad. Canadian forces should be able to respond to environmental or man made disasters. They should be capable of peacefully reinforcing police security and capable of responding to medical crises. Domestic forces would be concerned with border security as the primary means of defence, ensuring that traffic in and out of Canadian borders is of known affiliation.

Perhaps a non obvious example of such a dynamic domestic force would be a small fleet of arctic coast guard ships (3-5) that monitored the North West Passage. Currently there are unconfirmed allegations that certain countries are passing submarines through northern waters without making the Canadian government aware or asking permission. Similarly there are concerns of states making landfall on obscure northern islands. As global warming takes effect, the Canadian assets of the North West Passage, and the tremendous yet fragile resources of the north have become increasingly accessible. While equipped with surveillance capabilities (radar and sonar), such a fleet could simultaneously be utilized for scientific expeditions and research (tracking climate change for example). The fleets operations would be supplemented by a land based station that coordinated its actions and compiled all the information necessary to survey the North West Passage. Surely Canadian waters could be used by other states in times of emergency or as an occasional transportation route, but only with the Canadian government's permission and if appropriate, a cost for use. A coast guard and monitoring station while still functional would provide an ideal peaceful force to safeguard this valuable asset of Canada, to make sure that it is properly managed. Nunavut and the North West Territories, because of their size and sparse population density, intrinsically have problems with search and rescue operations in terms of area coverage and response time. A small fleet of long range, unmanned remote surveillance aircraft, based at the monitoring station would provide an effective service. Such aircraft could survey the uninhabited islands of the north, securing Canada's domestic sovereignty. They could also respond to search and rescue crises when needed, locating those in need and dropping essential supplies before rescuers arrive. This type of investment in a peaceful and dynamically functional force characterizes domestically what peacekeepers should abroad: a commitment to peace and security.

In the example of securing Canada's northern sovereignty by means of peaceful surveillance, what actions and policy would be in line with non hypocritical policy if a country's submarine was detected – without prior notice or permit – in the waters of the North West Passage? Clearly violent conflict or intimidation would not hold up to the standard of an exemplary state. The first thing that comes to the mind of one rooted in Middle power thinking is that this is the point in which the unrealistic idea of non-hypocritical action meets reality: that eventually violent force, or the threat thereof, may be necessary to prevail in international conflict. Bearing in mind that the currency of economic power garners more attention in a post-Cold war world than military might, and the idea that international legitimacy is an asset, solutions excluding force materialize. Asking the transgressing state for a commission while issuing a warning against further impositions could be an appropriate initial response. If non compliance ensues, certain peaceful methods of interdependent action exist: such as forwarding a UN Security Council resolution (a significantly extreme response), making an informal UN protest or remark; or issuing a boycott of tourist and non essential travel to the state in question. Ideally an international arbitrator, steeped in the premise of interdependence would make an impartial ruling on the case if the Canadian government brought the dispute to international court. The probability of these methods being successful is directly related to the legitimacy and vivacity of the United Nations, further elucidating its necessity.

A typical foreign policy decision – one that can be framed in terms of domestic security, legitimacy, interest, and hypocrisy – was made by Canada on Ballistic Missile Defence (BMD) in 2005. The debate over whether Canada should have joined BMD provides a clear case study of the kind of fundamental foreign policy decisions Canada has to make. A history of events and circumstances ultimately boiled down to an executive decision for Paul Martin: either 'yes' Canada would participate in the Bush Administration's program or 'no' it would not.

The story of BMD began in 1982 when then President Ronald Reagan announced his Strategic Defense Initiative (SDI), a plan to deploy a missile shield to protect America in case of a USSR nuclear strike. SDI's announcement did more than ruffle the feathers of the Soviet government, it violated the ABM treaty of 1972 between the US and USSR. The ABM treaty specifically banned any countermeasures to missile attacks: hence ensuring the possibility of mutually assured destruction. Reagan's program suffered from a complete lack of legitimacy, but if the shield worked –averting mutually assured destruction – then in theory it would be worth the risk. However, after billions of dollars of research and military spending, no effective shield was deployed. SDI simply did not work, and was scrapped. The only concrete results of Reagan's program were billions of dollars transferred from the taxpayer to those corporations contracted to unsuccessfully develop the technology. Successively, both President George Bush I, and Bill Clinton poured money into the drain that the idea of a missile shield became, with similar results.

Undeterred, George W. Bush has been no different from his predecessors, investing billions into a program that has yielded no results. One recent test of the technology cost 85 million dollars to perform and ended without anything leaving the launch pad. Despite such conspicuous failure, at the crux of the BMD debate is the fact that if ever a system were deployed, it could never be effective. The task of stopping a full fledged intercontinental ballistic missile attack is theoretically impossible. In order for a shield to be successful, it must shoot down all incoming missiles. Any country launching such an attack would launch missiles in the order of the hundreds, if not thousands. The thing is, not all of them have to be armed with a nuclear warhead: nine out of ten could be decoy duds indistinguishable from a real payload by satellite or radar. No matter how sophisticated, any shield could be overwhelmed by sheer volume. In fact, well before Martin rendered judgement (or stabbed in the dark) Russia had already declared that it possessed such shield penetrating techniques. At the highest level: offence will always trump defence, especially when the margin for error is zero. John Steinbruner in *Principles of Global Security* had this to say:

> It begins with a practical fact that, for all its unwelcome implications, cannot be denied: the array of technologies involved in nuclear weapons is much more readily applied to offensive than to defensive applications, so much so that a devastating assault cannot be physically precluded and therefore has to be convincingly dissuaded.[62] For the first time in history a society cannot be protected by interposing a barrier of military forces against potential sources of aggression, even if the society in question enjoys superior assets.[63]

It was in this context that Paul Martin was asked by George Bush to sign onto BMD. Many questioned why Bush needed to ask Canada for official partnership. Firstly through NORAD, Canada was already sharing aerial tracking information that could be used to identify incoming missiles by the United States over Canadian territory. Secondly, the United States was clearly not lacking either the financial support or military-industrial base to install such a shield. Finally the United States, if warned of an incoming missile towards say Chicago, passing over Manitoba, would not hesitate to shoot it down (if they developed such capacity) regardless of whether Canadian forces acquiesced or not – they would not have the time to ask nor would they think to. So why then, if the United States could have implemented the entire system with the same level of (in)effectiveness regardless of Canada's involvement or not, would George Bush, in his first official trip to Canada in November 2004, make a point in his speech to ask that Canada participate in US BMD? The United States was interested in the one asset that Canada possessed it did not: *legitimacy*.

What Bush was asking Martin to do however, was to forgo that legitimacy, to nullify it. By signing onto the program, Canada would not have increased the legitimacy of US BMD, as the Bush Administration hoped. Rather Canada would have dirtied its own legitimacy. BMD represents the purest form of the military industrial complex: the awarding of lucrative contracts, to military companies by government officials, for programs that serve no purpose and produce no results, except to endanger the very citizens who paid for them. Fortunately for Martin, the domestic support in Canada was lacking, specifically in Quebec where he hoped to improve his standings in the next election. Political ambition made the right decision for him. Martin officially announced Canada's non-involvement on March 22nd, 2005.

Clearly exemplary policies apply to the military in terms of what forces are invested in. Dynamic peacekeepers are ideal compared to antediluvian world war technology. But the true standard of how a state's military is measured of course, is how it is used. Most recently, Canada had a hand in the US led invasion of Afghanistan. Contrasting this was Canada's lack of participation in the US led invasion of Iraq. In the details of these two decisions, and under what circumstances they were made, is a case study for the erratic foreign policy behaviour Canada has exhibited since it began making its own decisions. Canada is far from being an exemplary state: the difference between these two decisions display the lack of a logical mandate.

To what category of action the US led invasion of Afghanistan belongs will differ depending on where one begins the story. If one began reading on September 11th, 2001 with the tremendous carnage and casualties inflicted upon innocent US citizens by Al-Qaeda terrorists: then the invasion of Afghanistan in order to depose the ruling Taliban regime would seem very much justified. Even certain things, such as 'precision' bombings that caused significant 'collateral damage' – the further loss of innocent lives, this time in Afghanistan – might be viewed as unfortunate but necessary, in light of the extreme damage the Taliban inflicted, and could potentially inflict in the future, both upon Afghanistan and the United States.

If one began reading the story earlier however, perhaps in 1979 when the USSR invaded Afghanistan, the transparent victimization of the United States clouds. In an example of the 'proxy' wars that marked the timeline of the Cold War, the United States – determined to contain the infectious spread of communist power – saw to it that the USSR's invasion of Afghanistan did not succeed. In order to do so, the US government backed anti-communists forces in the form of the Mujahadeen –a group made up of the likes of Osama Bin Laden – providing them with funding and sophisticated arms. The USSR invasion turned into a deep quagmire and was eventually repelled. The militants then seized power, consequently impoverishing the citizens of Afghanistan and creating shelter for Al-Qaeda before the US finally, at a cost, deposed them, with the help of Canada, in 2001.

Both the victims of the September 11th attacks and of the US bombings of Afghanistan had no part in the decisions to back the US led invasion of Afghanistan in 2001, the September 11th attacks, the USSR decision to invade Afghanistan in 1979, or the US response to back the militants that drove them out. The US and USSR governments, Al-Qaeda and Osama Bin Laden himself, where the decision makers, the groups that set the chain of events in motion. Missing from this list is the Canadian government or Canadian citizens.

On an individual level, one cannot but feel anguish and sorrow at the loss of life on September 11th. On an individual level, Canadians mourned for those who lost their lives, and contributed time, effort and money to the families of the victims. For the Canadian politician, displaying anguish for the loss of life is not analogous to believing one must send Canadians to kill and be killed in Afghanistan in order to uproot the Taliban, a militant government that owed its reign of power to the United States itself. The question for Canada in the wake of September 11th was not whether to participate in a war that was about to begin with the invasion of Afghanistan. It was not to determine if this new war, this war about to commence, was *just* or not. No new war began in 2001 with the first Afghani child dying unwittingly from an American bomb. The question for Canada was whether or not to enter a seemingly perpetual war. An exemplary state would have never backed a mercenary force to fight the USSR. An exemplary state would never abet a country in the bombing of a population. Therefore Canada, if interested in real (opposed to relative) legitimacy, should not have participated in the invasion of Afghanistan. Romantic Canadian politicians sending soldiers to hunt the US manifested Taliban in the caves of Afghanistan: a foolish decision. By doing so, Canada effectively declared that the hypocritical policy, the bellicose hegemony, that placed the United States in such a position was in the first place, justified.

To confer legitimacy upon any international action, approval from an impartial international body is needed. The three tenets of contemporary legitimate peacekeeping and peacemaking are: "Consent, Impartiality, and Minimum use of force"[64]. Bombing, being an act of terrorism, is a bludgeoning tactic far removed from the minimally necessary force. Though the majority Afghani citizens may have hoped for the eventual extraction of the Taliban regime, few I would suspect would agree to their own deaths in exchange. Nothing is to say that Canada could not have helped stabilize the country, by means of peacekeeping, in the aftermath of US military action, if Afghani consent was procured, if impartiality was maintained, if minimum force was invoked. In fact, an impartial and legitimate state that possessed a dynamic peacekeeping force would be ideally suited to ensure that a new government formed in the invasion's aftermath represented the people of Afghanistan. As America has demonstrated, a power seeking to occupy a country after invading it has significant inherent obstacles in achieving this goal.

The war in Iraq does not seem far removed in circumstance from Afghanistan in that it was not a new war that began in 2003 with US invasion. Rather it is the latest chapter in perpetual US war, with an ambiguous beginning and an end beyond any foreseeable horizon. Perhaps it began in 1991 with the US led repulsion of Saddam's invasion of Kuwait. Or in 1998, or in 1993 with US bombing campaigns. Perhaps it began in 1980, when the US supported Saddam Hussein in his war against Iran. Afghanistan and Iraq: did Canada recognize that one was a perpetual war while improperly identifying the other, or were the decisions made based on the future political fortunes of men seeking to thrive in a faulty electoral system?

The United States does not enjoy any degree of exception from the exemplary state thesis: it is a country like any other. While its form is the same, its impact upon Canada is greater than that of any other state. The United States is the only country that Canada borders geographically, and is Canada's largest trading partner. Canada's economy is hence intertwined to a high degree with that of the United States, a connection reinforced by the North American Free Trade Agreement (NAFTA). Furthermore, the United States possesses the world's largest economy, and is by far the most powerful country, enjoying superiority in both economic and traditional military strength. In judging how Canada should interact with the United States – just as with relations between every other country – Canada must ask 'What world does Canada want?' Answering the question provides the goals which can be applied via the principles of the exemplary state. Because of proximity and modern developments, high volumes of interaction take place between the two countries: in immigration, culture, information, and social dialogues for example. It is clear that some of these interactions are relevant to the policies that Canada should implement as they affect such goals as peace, prosperity, and the ubiquity of fundamental human rights. Of course some of these interactions do not affect these goals, or the goals that Canadian policy makers have in general and therefore should not be regarded as relevant to policy. Finally through developments in modernity, certain interactions that have always existed, such as those between the air above the two states, have increased in importance.

In analyzing what policies to implement, what course of action, and tone of dialogue to pursue with respect to the United States, Canada must also ask 'What world does the US want?' Canada should not answer this question for any country; rather, Canada should evaluate what world the US is striving for, based on observance of its actions (not rhetoric). This assumes that the actions of the United States are meant to be exemplary, that as a country it desires the world to emulate its pattern of behaviour, that it is setting an example. If the conclusion reached in analyzing these actions turns out to be harmonious with the world Canada desires, then cooperation and agreement with the policies of the US would be in order. If however, these actions show an affinity for a world that is different, or the opposite of what ideals Canada seeks, then it would be inadvisable – indeed it would be hypocritical – for Canada to act in parallel with the US on those actions. What is important in this evaluation is a lack of default answers. Historically Canada has been a harbinger of anti-American sentiment, primarily as a result of the large immigration of embittered loyalists to Canada after the American Declaration of Independence. A stagnant opinion is foolish. Perpetually Canada must reconsider what path the United States' actions are following and whether that path is the one Canada wishes to walk. One must consistently re-analyze any actor, for example with the question "has the United States become an exemplary state?" If ever the question where to be answered in the affirmative, Canada would be blind to still hold its default position. In analyzing what world the US currently, through its actions, wants, let us look outside of the exemplary state conception.

Robert Cooper, a senior British diplomat, describes the current world to have three forms of state: pre-modern, modern, and post-modern. Firstly the: "traditional 'modern' states… behave as states always have, following interest, power and raison d'état."[65] In terms of military strength, for these modern states: "this is still a world in which the ultimate guarantor of security is force"[66]. However having emerged, and for the first time in human history, "are post-imperial, post-modern states which no longer think of security primarily in terms of conquest."[67] For these post-modern states and opposed to their modern counterparts, "force is rejected as a way of settling disputes."[68]

The propensity to use force and the goal of increasing power is not the only thing that separates a modern state from a post-modern one. To Cooper, the endorsement of universal human rights, as well as the existence of democracy and capitalism within a state are requisite for it to be considered post-modern. Greatly uninhibited trade and migration of people between post-modern states as well as border relationships that rely on trust and interdependence are also important qualities defining his post-modernism. There is also an open policy between post-modern states about the number and location of Weapons of Mass Destruction, which is reassuring. However, there is a flaw in the post-modern system, and it arises when one must confront another country who does not play by the post-modern rules of interdependent security. The problem is, post-modernism is a voluntary thing, and if a country such as Israel does not want to play by post-modern rules, then there is going to be a problem interacting with it. When such a case occurs, post-modern states may defect from their noble values. Again, they would never take violent action against another post-modern state, but when dealing with the barbarism of a modern or pre-modern state, which does not seem rational, the post-modern may too become irrational according to Cooper. An example of this behaviour would be the United Kingdom's (a post-modern state to Cooper) participation in the invasion of Iraq in 2003, also a hypocritical action.

So where do Canada and the United States fit into this conceptualization? Included in the list of post-modern countries are: those in the European Union, Sweden and Japan. "Outside Europe, Canada is certainly a post-modern state"[69] Cooper contends. Perhaps Cooper is not fully aware of Canada's non compliance with UN resolutions. Perhaps he chalks Canada's involvement in Haiti, Afghanistan and Kosovo to the problems that post-modern states have when interacting with the pre modern. Perhaps Canada is simply post-modern, when compared to other states. What is not clear to him, however, is the categorization of the United States:

> The USA is the more doubtful case [for post-modernism] since it is not clear that the US government or Congress accepts either the necessity or desirability of interdependence, or its corollaries of openness, mutual surveillance and mutual interference, to the same extent as most European governments now do.

The United States possesses some post-modern beliefs to Cooper: the liberalization of trade through NAFTA and a stated commitment to democracy. One could question the democracy that exists in a system with two identical parties. Protectionist trade policies would also seem to undermine the idea of trade liberalization. The use of force and desire to dominate other states through force further unequivocally preclude the US from being so categorized however. Using Cooper's system of grouping countries is not to say that it is the correct or most comprehensive system of understanding states. Maps written in black, white and one shade of grey are of limited use. It does however provide a contrast between the United States and Canada through its categorizations that the exemplary state thesis cannot. Canada and the US are both hypocritical states in that conception.

Cooper's conceptualization can also chart the direction in which countries are changing (progressive, stagnant, deteriorating). So if a country has displayed a tendency to favour post modern behaviour, thinking in terms of interdependence as opposed to conquest, it can be seen as moving in a positive direction. A state however can deteriorate from modern, to pre-modern. Third world failed states typify pre-modern classifications. Since the break up of the Soviet Union, the resulting burdens placed on Russia have exuded constant pressure, threatening such deterioration.

In Canada, some of Cooper's post-modern beliefs are thought to be emerging: openness of military strength and location of military resources, an increasing domestic commitment to some human and minority rights, the development of a fairer and more equal opportunity economy, and an investment in progressive social programs. By this conceptualization, Canada could definitely become a post-modern state given some changes. Again, there are some patterns of behaviour the United States has exhibited, that fundamentally disqualify it from being considered a candidate for leaving modern tendencies behind in favour of post-modernism. International military hegemony is one, over countries across the globe: from Nicaragua and Panama, to Iraq and Afghanistan, to Sudan and the Congo, to Kosovo and Vietnam. A lack of openness about its military is another, including on Weapons of Mass Destruction and Ballistic Missile Defence specifically, but more generally pertaining to all high technology weaponry in US possession. A third nonnegotiable tenet disqualifying post-modernism is domestic policies that are in violation of fundamental human rights, such as the death penalty, and detention and imprisonment without trial. Finally, a lack of interdependence (isolationism) can be exemplified by not accepting peaceful interdependence in: not agreeing to the International Land Mine Ban, not ratifying the Kyoto

Accord, not joining The International Criminal Court, and continually veto-ing UN Security Council resolutions that decry hostile US military and/or covert actions. Through the discrepancies in post-modern and modern, one can see that to Cooper, Canada and the United States do not possess the same vision of how the world should fundamentally operate. However, whether there is actually a fundamental divergence in Canada and the United States' desires is unclear. If there was, it would be hypocritical of Canada to collude with and tacitly approve certain US actions.

Today the US provides Canada with markets for primary industries and resources, from oil and beef, to lumber and raw metals, to electricity and ap-ples. Companies like Ford and Chrysler, that originated in the United States often employ Canadian workers for automobile production. Hollywood films often take advantage of the cities of Canada. The United States' strong economy is inextricably linked to that of Canada's. This has created pressure for Canadian policy makers to approve the actions of the United States in general: to have a default opinion. What should be most clear is the way in which Canada communicates with the United States. If Canada's ideals are not harmonious with the US, if Canada's prescribed solution is polar oppo-site, the US must be clearly informed. A decision on involvement in a US war should not come to US policy makers over televised news: it should come from Canadian policy makers in a clear, rational statement.

The results of dissidence, some say, are clear. When unmitigated free trade is allowed to occur between states of asymmetrical power, what one can assume will happen is that the more powerful state will dominate the less powerful one if given the chance. The rich elite of the more powerful country will exploit the poor of the less powerful country if no barrier against such oppression exists. What becomes apparent then, is that a strong, comprehen-sive mutual dispute resolution mechanism between asymmetrical powers is essential to ensuring a fair trading relationship, especially for the less power-ful state. If the price of dissidence is exploitation through a trade agreement, then it is clear that the relationship between states of asymmetrical power is not interdependent; rather, the more powerful state is dominating the less. If when the trade agreement was conceived however, there was a dispute resolu-tion mechanism that was impartial, robust, and comprehensive, that clearly stated the fundamental equality between states of unequal strengths when they disagreed then: the price of dissidence would be purely political, not economic. Disputes would be resolved impartially. It is clear now, that the NAFTA had no such dispute resolution mechanism, probably because it was conceived by modern states, one wishing to enhance its perceived middle power status, the other further hoarding its supremacy. If interdependent economic activity for the benefit of all was the goal, and security through trust – through post-modern ideals – was the overarching principle governing such an agreement, rules would be followed. Rules would also be followed by exemplary states.

The standard of Canada's foreign policy is its applications to the actions and policies of the United States. If Canada's foreign policy is to be 'inspiring world peace' as opposed to aspiring to be a middle power, then that should be reflected in Canada's relationships with all countries, including the United States. The fact that the US is imposing and powerful is just further reason to encourage it to be peaceful, progressive, and multilateral. Canada can choose to encourage the United States to be a peaceful, respectful member of the world community and choose to remain distinct in policy and economy from that of the United States. If Canada chooses so, Canada has the chance to set an example for the rest of the world that asymmetrical powers can co-exist without the less power compromising its policy. If Canadian foreign policy goals are not well represented in relations with the United States, if Canadian commitment to human rights for example, is understated, or not stated clearly to the United States when it needs to be clearly stated the most, then it will be infinitely more difficult for Canada to claim *legitimacy*. Though there are a variety of pressures bearing down from the United States, Canada's foreign policy will be able to stand on its own if policy makers display the will to let it. More inextricable is the link between the countries' environments.

Because some of Canada's past foreign policy choices were void of rationality by no means impairs the ability of future decisions to be nuanced and logical. Because Canada has acted hypocritically in the past, does not exempt the chances it could become an exemplary state in the future. In order to do so however, Canada cannot have it both ways. Canada cannot be concerned with maintaining a legitimate image while endorsing and benefiting from, illegitimate actions. Canada cannot ignore the UN resolutions that have been passed against it, such as the 1998 resolution that correctly identified the public funding of Catholic secondary schools as discriminatory. In addition to such resolutions, the United Nations Human Rights Committee has repeatedly berated Canada for: its anti-terrorist legislation that allows the deportation of immigrants without trial or evidence, slow processing of First Nation land claims, non documentation and non prevention of violence against First

Nation women, allowing male correctional officers to guard female prisoners, and imprisoning those with mental illness when there is a shortage of institutional housing capacity. The imprisonment of individuals domestically for years without trial is similarly troubling. A state has no legitimacy in insisting another state endorses the universal human rights prescribed by the UN while ignoring them at home. Canada is not an exemplary state because it has fewer hypocritical actions to its name than other states. When compared to other countries Canada has *relative*, not *real* legitimacy.

How do you convince someone born in the rich 20% of the world that their life is of the same worth as someone born in the poor 80%? In discussing the current world order, it was mentioned that some would argue Canada benefits from the current order where this divide exists. I did not endorse this not because I don't believe Canada is part of the rich 20% that is actively oppressing the poor 80%. Canada is. I did not endorse the idea because I do not think that it is in anyone's *best* interests for there to be such a dynamic. It may be in Canada's *better* interest, better to have a gluttonous economy with a world of terrorist threats and third world instability than to have one's economy overrun. But *best* implies optimal. It is in Canada's (and every other state's) *best* interests for all states to enjoy a degree of prosperity. In trusting, interdependent prosperity states can find security, in prosperity that relies on hegemony, states can expect perpetual violent conflict.

Another way of thinking of how an exemplary state would form policies; as opposed to the setting of an example, 'being the change it wants to see in the world' idea, would be eschewing the type actions that are the converse of exemplary: hypocritical ones. A policy devoted solely to evil would be incorrectly described as hypocritical. As Canada has demonstrated, and as the United States exemplifies, to posses policy that is hypocritical, one must take some actions that seem altruistic, and some that seem selfish, in nature. Currently, Canadian foreign policy has seen flashes of both exemplary and hypocritical action while advertising only the existence of the former. In that sense, Canada has been a wolf in sheep's clothing.

5

Sustainability, sustainability everywhere:
and still the air stinks

"The case for reform that I have tried to make is not based on altruism, nor on saving nature for its own sake. I happen to believe these are moral imperatives, but such arguments cut against the grain of human desire. The most compelling reason for reforming the system is that the system is in no one's interest. It is a suicide machine." [70]

– Ronald Wright's "A Short History of Progress"
on civilization's need for long term thinking and
environmental sustainability based on past failed civilizations

"Imagine, for a moment, a world where fossil fuels are no longer burned to generate power, heat, or light. A world no longer threatened by global warming or geopolitical conflict in the Middle East. A world where every person on earth has access to electricity. That world now looms on the horizon." [71]

– Jeremy Rifkin, "The Dawn of the Hydrogen Economy"

The sustainability of the environment will become the most important issue Canadian and world society faces, at some point in the future. Today it is not. In the 2004 Canadian federal election, the Liberal and Conservative parties – the frontrunners – barely mentioned that there was an environment. The only time either made an empty environmental commitment was when prompted by the NDP, Bloq, or media. During the Bush-Kerry race of 2004, environmental issues were barely mentioned, and rightly so. Neither candidate had any idea about the environment, or his party's policy towards it. Brought up once in a debate[72], each candidate prattled about how their plan would ensure the environment flourished: perhaps assuaging the layman who cares about, but is not driven to heavily research, environmental policy. The environment is an area of public policy in which emulation of trends in American policy would not in general, be in Canada's best interests. Effects of American environmental policies are hard to calculate in relative importance to Canada because a significant portion of the pollution the Canadian population is exposed to originates in the United States. As Trudeau once quipped, "Canada is a country whose main exports are hockey players and cold fronts. Our main imports are baseball players and acid rain." Pollution in similar fashion to a variety of new concerns to the globalized world of the 21st century ignores borders[73]. And yet it is clear that currently, a sane environment policy is not crucial or even remotely requisite to gaining power in North American politics.

First let us consider, what is the environment? The environment is everything surrounding us, which could be inclusive of everything. However, the consensus of mainstream 'environmentalists' would agree in defining the environmental struggle as the search for, and implementation of one thing: sustainability[74]. That is the ability of the earth, and its ecosystems to sustain: the natural climate (with an absence of manmade global warming or ozone hole, with no resulting increase in natural disasters), natural resources (abundant clean water, clean air, healthy soil), and natural life or biodiversity (flowers, trees, bunnies, tigers and bears). Put another way, any iterative process that consumes resources over time – such as making cars, growing crops, or living in a house – can be defined as sustainable if it can be repeatedly indefinitely without modification. Currently Canadians are not living in a sustainable system of existence. If everyone on the planet lived with the level of consumption and waste that the average Canadian does, mankind would need 4 earths[75]. This may or may not be a useful statement beyond setting a tone of magnitude. Apart from being a fundamental societal issue, the environment provides a primary example of the interconnectedness of our lives, and how factors in change are both exponential and interdependent. A typifying example of these ideas at work is found in biodiversity.

Let us imagine that a previously sparsely populated region of the North West Territories is newly occupied by an oil drilling and refinery operation; made possible by new technology that more easily pierces permafrost and gains access to the valued resources below. The economic success of the operation promotes ripple effect job growth and the local citizens delight in their flourishing economy. The Yellowknife airport receives more traffic; jobs are created for refinery and drilling workers as well as in secondary areas like housing, food services, and health care. Furthermore, due to the geographic proximity to the Albertan and American markets (compared to the Middle East), the oil company regards this new investment as an economically maintainable source of revenue, and wishes to maximize its potential by building a pipeline from the operation to southern infrastructure, creating even more jobs. All of this economic growth is due to a new technology that made a previously non-cost-effective drilling, cost-effective.

There are disadvantages however. The main refinery complex is located on the Mackenzie River, which acts as a heat sink and chemical waste disposal. When the river is polluted by the excess heat and chemical by-products of the refining process, the local fish population begins to die out. An inability to live at even slightly higher temperatures, combined with the poisonous chemicals now in the river, reduces their population by 40%. The fish that do survive become carriers of the fat-soluble chemicals in their (high fat) bodies. The local polar bear population enjoys eating fish as an appetizer to seal whenever possible. However, polar bears eating fish is not a linear relationship, as a bear usually likes to have more than one. Consequently the chemicals from consumed fish accumulate in the bears, resulting in deteriorating states of health for those that do not die of poisoning over time. Of course this trend continues, for now that the polar bear population is reduced, other prey, namely seals but also reindeer and rodents have population explosions. This results in a larger reindeer population consuming more vegetation, and a larger seal population eating more fish. These new stresses on the fish and vegetation of the ecosystem result in their decimation.

The maintenance of biodiversity is very relevant in the maintenance of an ecosystem, and provides transparent insight into the effects of disrupting equilibrium. It is a quintessential example of why the environment should be stewarded with such care: the loss of one species – one part of the equation – can yield tumultuous results for the rest of the system. The environment and environmental sustainability is exemplary in the discussion of interconnectedness and exponential effects in society for a variety of reasons. For one: sustainable solutions have to be implemented in all areas of society to be effective. Citizens have to be made aware of environmental issues, and if properly informed will elect governments that place the environment in a necessary position of priority. Governments have to pass laws that protect the environment (and hence citizens) as well as protecting businesses and corporations from being placed in compromising positions (for example choosing between strong fourth quarter profits and chemical dumping). Finally, everyone benefits from a healthy environment: everyone breathes air and drinks water, and everyone needs to eat to survive.

With this in mind it becomes obvious that environmental issues are not just the concern of 'environmentalists'. Demonstrating this is the eclectic range of places in which environmental concerns surface. Take for example, a discussion of ideas on meeting Kyoto Protocol commitments found in the

Canadian Medical Associated Journal. An editorial in said publication highlighted, "the intimate connection between the state of the environment and the state of our health."[76] A simpler statement of interrelationships could not be found: doctors care about the environment because an unhealthy environment makes people sick. The year 2005 saw 5800 smog related deaths in Ontario alone[77]. Not only does a vested interest in the health of a population make doctors aware of issues like pollution and climate change, it also makes them politically motivated. In an article in the same journal, two professors state: "The commitments made by the governments in signing the Kyoto Protocol are not sufficient to tackle climate change."[78] The authors of a comprehensive study on peacekeeping cited earlier, in chapter four, included in their discussion of the globalized world the idea that: "Potentially tectonic transformations are also underway in the global commons (in the climatic system, the atmosphere, the oceans and the polar regions) and pollutants (such as acid rain and toxic and nuclear wastes) show scant regard for political boundaries."[79]The notion that the environment is a pervasive issue to the extent that it has contributed to the prevalent paradigm of peacekeeping is another sign that perhaps the term 'environmentalists' should apply to people in ubiquity. More than even human health, geopolitics provides insight into the necessity for citizens to care about their environment. In a New York Times editorial that wondered why George W. Bush had not taken a proactive environmental approach as President, despite the overwhelming scientific evidence of a threat from global warming, Pulitzer Prize winner Thomas Friedman made this causal connection: "By doing nothing to lower U.S. oil consumption, we are financing both sides in the war on terrorism and strengthening the worst governments in the world."[80]

Realizing the interconnectedness of the environment, any solutions initiated to curb and reverse the trends that have resulted in its degradation must be holistic in approach. When seeking to reduce greenhouse gasses, it is inadvisable to focus singularly on the emissions of the automobile industry with government regulations. An effective solution would entail reducing all variables in the equation: power plants, industrial processes, and transportation. A holistic approach creates a few benefits. For one, to achieve the desired results, a minimum is required of each variable in terms of performance. Let us hypothetically say that in Canada per year, the non electricity-producing industries (such as mining and manufacturing) account for 100 mega tonnes (Mt) of greenhouse gas emissions, power plants account for another 100Mt, and that the automobile and transportation industries account for a third 100Mt. If policy makers were to regulate just the transportation industry, asking them to reduce emissions to a level of 88Mt, a couple things might happen. One is that the transportation industry would rightly feel that it is being singled out by the government: that its competitiveness was being unfairly impaired, an opinion lobbyists and lawyers would make sure policy makers were aware of. The second is that, even if the transportation industry tapered their emissions to 88 Mt: the other two sectors, without similar regulation could have naturally increased their emissions to 102Mt each, under the same time span. So while the government set a goal of 288 Mt, the end of the day reality could be 292 Mt. However, if regulations obliged all three sectors to reduce their emissions to 96 Mt each, the same end result of 288Mt could be achieved, and no industry would stray. Only in this scenario, the bottom line burden placed on an individual sector is mitigated, and complaints about discrimination would be unfounded. This solution moves all variables in the equation of greenhouse gas emissions in the desired direction, with expected secondary effects of less smog days, and deaths due to asthma: resulting in tertiary effects of less health care dollars spent on treating asthma and so on. Positive change in all variables (as opposed to one) that affect a system has a number of benefits: it ensures that there are no discounted factors able to move in the opposite direction, while the strain put upon the system in individual areas is minimized by diversified pressure.

Regulations and Ideology

A solution is so often discounted as an option by those who espouse a rigid ideology. Many self labelled "leftists" claim that corporations are out to destroy the environment, to rape and pillage it in order to make the highest possible profits. This is not true. There is no necessary correlation between making profits, and damaging the environment. It is not necessarily true that a corporation will make more money (in the short, middle, or long term) if it engages in unsustainable business practices. It is true that a corporation (especially a publicly traded one) will try, under the current legal and economic system, to make decisions that yield the largest profit. However, if the legal and economic system were designed in such a way that it would always be detrimental to the profit of a corporation if it engaged in unsustainable business practices – then by capitalist instinct – any successful corporation would naturally lean towards implementing the most environmentally friendly solutions. There is nothing inherent in the definition of 'corporation' that makes it an enemy of the environment or anything else: that characteristic is dependant upon the system within which it does business.

On the other side of the popularity contest, many self labelled "rightists" reason that the elimination of regulation, or 'red tape', to the maximal extent will create the most positive and dynamic marketplace, and in turn the most salubrious environment for all people to prosper. This conception seems to be directly contradicted by the fact that the primary method of achieving capital – through the stock market – is solely based on regulation and law that the government has instituted. The current legal characteristics of today's publicly traded company: no limit on the number of shareholders, no limit on the level of investment in the company (assuming its not a monopoly), a separation of power between owner (shareholders) and operator (CEO), and most importantly no liability for stockowners beyond their initial investment, is maintained by the laws and regulations of governments. Without government intervention, one hundred equally endowed shareholders of a company owing one hundred million dollars could be liable for one million dollars each, even if their initial investment was ten dollars. However, under current government regulation each shareholder merely loses their ten dollar investment, the company is dissolved pending bankruptcy, and either the one hundred million dollars is paid by the bankruptcy insurance company, the government, a combination of the two, or it is not paid back at all. This system of regulation has created the dynamic that is the current capitalist market because its limited liability encourages investment (and therefore growth) with a predefined floor level of risk, while maintaining the absence of a ceiling on an investment's possible return.

If one form of regulation (such as the structure of liability and investment found in the stock market) can create a marketplace where production and profit is maximized, then cannot regulation create a marketplace where production and profit is maximized within standards of ethicality? It already has. It is currently unethical and illegal for a business to do a certain number of things outside of a framework that government regulation has created. For example a business cannot kill people, own or sell people, or loan children out for sexual intercourse. A business can also not do things that are relatively minor, like employ those who are under a certain age if that business serves alcohol. A business cannot exaggerate or be duplicitous about its earnings, taxes owed, or overhead. If these things occur, then a business is typically punished in a manner severe enough that it was not profitable for the unethical practice to have been adopted (for example by means of a fine, audit, criminal investigation and prosecution, or class action lawsuit). There are always grey areas in such laws, but the regulations do exist and are accepted: no contemporary business groans about no longer being able to own people.

If a regulatory structure has created a marketplace where production and profits are maximized within the rules of the law, cannot those rules be extended to ensure that the marketplace has a long term future? Cannot those laws protect and insulate the marketplace from proceeding in a direction that in the long term is unsustainable? Cannot those regulations dissuade the marketplace from behaviour that will inevitably not be in its own best interests: behaviour that will inevitably lead to its downfall? Just as capital gained from business that profited from killing citizens would be unsustainable, and therefore in the eventual term, unprofitable (and unethical), so too is capital gained from businesses that threaten either in whole or in part the system of life on this planet, because in the eventual term if the system of life degrades beyond a certain point, it may not be in the best interests of those making profit. It may not be cost effective for those making profit: if the resources the marketplace relied upon shore up, if the citizens that made up the marketplace a business profited from suffer from famine, if the system by which shareholders procure their profit margin is not sustainable.

Quantifying Sustainability

There are many studies available that provide a framework for the discussion of progress in an environmental context. For a variety of reasons, one study providing a strong launching point is the ESI, or Environmental Sustainability Index published by Yale University.[81] The ESI is a comprehensive ranking of country's environmental sustainability, covering 146 countries. It understands that a multitude of (associated) factors affect the environment, tracking 76 factors in 5 more closely relatable areas. It quantifies these factors, making precise and definable goals for governments easily available. Furthermore it is auspiciously respectable, not only for being published out of Yale University, but also for being released and recognized at the World Economic Forum: a favourable crossover for 'environmentalists'. Finally, it is namely concerned with the primary goal of environmentalism: sustainability. Out of the 146 countries documented, Canada ranked 6th, and the United States 45th.[82] The top five were Finland, Norway, Uruguay, Sweden, and Iceland, respectively. Countries like Gabon, Mali, Bhutan, Botswana, and Panama, were all ranked ahead of the United States. The ESI also recognized the environmental link between Canada and the United States, placing them in the same group of 8 similar countries.

As mentioned, the ESI documents 5 closely correlated categories of factors, they are: Global Stewardship, Reducing Stresses, Reducing Human Vulnerability, Social and Institutional Capacity, and Environmental Systems. Each of the five categories had a maximum score of 100. On Global

Stewardship, Canada scored 21, compared with 45, 77, 81, and 85 in the other four categories. Global Stewardship will be the sole category discussed, both in the interest of brevity and because many of the factors contributing to Canada's low score in the area are endemic and fundamental to Canada's current inability to forge a sustainable future. One variable contributing to Global Stewardship was "reducing transboundary Environmental pressures", which was the amalgam of two factors: "Sulphur dioxide (SO2) exports" and the "import of polluting goods and raw materials as percentage of total imports of goods and services". This was by far where Canada scored the worst. Further important factors in the Global Stewardship score of 21 were "Greenhouse Gas [GHG] emissions", and "International Collaborative Efforts", which broke down further into "Carbon emissions per capita", "Carbon emissions per million US dollars GDP" in addition to "Number of memberships in environmental intergovernmental organizations", and "Contribution to international and bilateral funding of environmental projects and development aid", and "Participation in international environmental agreements", respectively.

The commonality in all these esoteric titles – under whose measurements Canada fared miserably – is that their conditions would be drastically improved by Canada meeting the stated goals of the Kyoto Protocol: yes, that international agreement Jack Layton is constantly yelling menacingly at people about. Though Canada, under the Liberal party's direction has signed onto the treaty which nobly commits countries to reduce their greenhouse gas emissions, to a goal of 6% below 1990 levels, it has done little to attain this goal. In fact between 1990 and 2002, Canadian greenhouse gas emissions have increased over 20%, and the trend is not slowing down, never mind reversing. By the year 2010, annual greenhouse gas emissions in Canada are expected to be in the range of 800Mt, while the goals set by the Kyoto Protocol call for a reduction to 570Mt (See Figure 5.1). Moreover, though reaching the goals of the Kyoto Protocol would help bolster Canada's scores in Global Stewardship, as well as mitigate environmental problems; it alone will not solve the problem of climate change. Reaching Kyoto goals would merely leave Canada in a position to begin to make a serious difference about the environment and climate change more specifically. Troubling in Canada's equation is the position of the United States.

Fig 5.1: Canadian Emissions Trend and Forecast 1990-2010.[83]

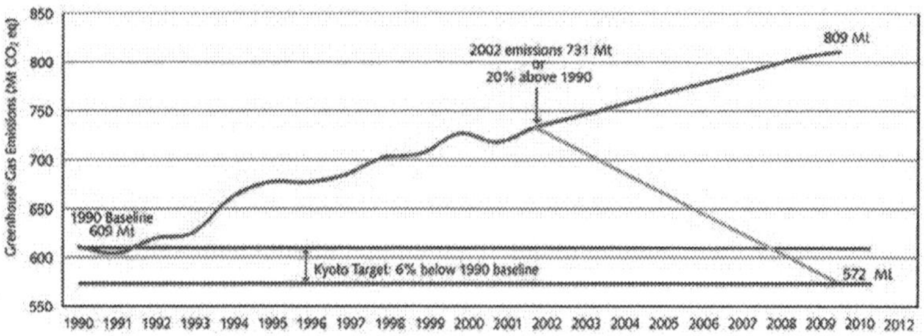

The environmental policy of the United States' government is so far removed from the analysis of its own scientific community that it can only be described as laughable. Though the Bush Administration is responsible for a swathe of revoked and neutered environmental regulations; those related to climate change are perhaps the most unconcealed. George Bush's stated reasons why the United States did not sign onto the Kyoto Protocol illustrate this: "Had we joined the Kyoto Treaty it would have cost America a lot of jobs. It's one of these deals where in order to be popular in the halls of Europe you sign a treaty. There's a better way to do it. The quality of air is cleaner since I've been the president of the US."[84]. It is interesting that George Bush can make such a statement: that the air is cleaner since he has been in office. Though the 43rd President has lied outright, he does not do it very often, and he did not technically lie in this case. The qualification that afforded him the ability to make such a statement is found in the recent redefinition of what constitutes air pollution in the United States. If a pollutant that made up 20% or 30%, for example, of the total air pollution in your country, suddenly and discontinuously evaporated from the list of air pollutants, you could claim that the air has become 20% to 30% cleaner since you were President. Which pollutant did the United States federal government (specifically the Environmental Protection Agency, EPA) decide to take off that list? Believe it or not, it was Carbon Dioxide (CO_2), which by referring to Figure 5.2, one can see made up substantially more than 20% to 30%. A strategic, yet not exactly subtly shrewd move considering that the United States had a worse ESI Greenhouse gas score than even Canada, and is far and away the world's largest polluter. And yet Canada's Greenhouse gas emissions, while receiving a slightly better rating than the US in the ESI, are increasing faster in the post Kyoto period.

There were differences of opinion in those responding to the EPA's decision. "Why would you regulate a pollutant that is an inert gas that is vital to plant photosynthesis and that people exhale when they breathe?" argued Eron Shosteck, a spokesman for the Alliance of Automobile Manufacturers, a Washington-based industry lobby. "That's not a pollutant."[85] "Refusing to call greenhouse-gas emissions a pollutant is like refusing to say that smoking causes lung cancer," responded Melissa Carey, a climate policy specialist for Environmental Defense, a New York-based environmental group.[86]. For reference, the idea that CO2 was not a pollutant was also in direct contradiction to a precedent set in a 1998 position taken by the Clinton Administration.[87]

Figure 5.2: U.S. Anthropogenic Greenhouse Gas Emissions by Gas, 2001.[88] (Million Metric Tons of Carbon Equivalent)

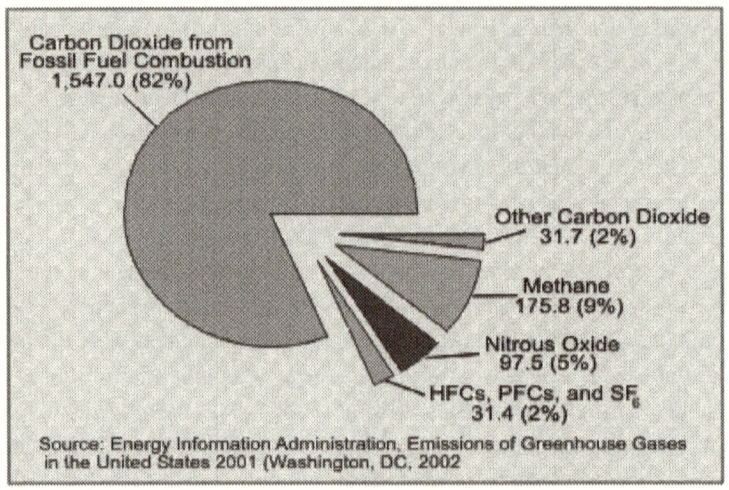

Carbon Dioxide from Fossil Fuel Combustion 1,547.0 (82%)

Other Carbon Dioxide 31.7 (2%)

Methane 175.8 (9%)

Nitrous Oxide 97.5 (5%)

HFCs, PFCs, and SF$_6$ 31.4 (2%)

Source: Energy Information Administration, Emissions of Greenhouse Gases in the United States 2001 (Washington, DC, 2002)

One of the cited reasons the United States did not ratify the Kyoto Protocol was that there was no proof that carbon dioxide was a pollutant, or contributing to the greenhouse effect and climate change. The majority of high school students who studied chemistry, biology, or geography beginning in 1970 to today could explain that carbon dioxide contributes to global warming; it is pretty simple. Here is a basic lesson in the earth's climate. First, the more carbon dioxide (or other GHG) in the upper atmosphere, the more the earth will heat up. The reason for this being that carbon dioxide traps sunlight from escaping the atmosphere when reflected. When the sun shines on the earth a percentage of the light is reflected both off the earth's surface and off clouds, back into outer space. However, the greater the percent of carbon dioxide in the atmosphere, the less sunlight that will escape by means of reflection because it is trapped: thus heating up the earth. The reason this is called the greenhouse effect, is because in effect the earth becomes a giant greenhouse, carbon dioxide acts in a similar fashion to a greenhouse's glass roof.

Where do the majority of carbon dioxide emissions originate? Deforestation, volcanic activity, and forest fires all have impact. Deforestation impacts the natural cycle of photosynthesis and respiration, and the continued loss of forests may remove the chances for a sustainable solution to climate change. Prior to industrialization, animal respiration and plant photosynthesis, which are chemically symbiotic, were relatively balanced. When an animal breathes in oxygen ($O2$) it is absorbed into the blood stream, and it breathes out carbon dioxide ($CO2$) as a product of this respiration. When a plant conducts photosynthesis (the process by which plants produce sugar for nourishment), it takes in carbon dioxide as a reactant, and produces oxygen.[89] Hence two dominant forms of life existed, relying on each other in balance. This equilibrium has been disrupted as deforestation has severely reduced plant capacity in the equation. Between the years 1200 and 2000, world forest coverage has been estimated to have been reduced from 6.0 billion hectares to 3.6 billion hectares[90]. The crux of deforestation is reversing its impact; trees grow slowly, and current rates of consumption are clearly unsustainable.

Unprovoked forest fires are another interesting note in the equation of climate change. Fires will occur naturally in forests to help maintain a balance; certain organisms stand to gain from a small fire. Decomposers such as grubs, fungi, moss, and termites will benefit from consuming the remains of dead trees that have fallen during a fire. Similarly, older and larger trees that survive a fire will benefit from the natural fertilizer the charred remains of cleared out brush provide. However, since human provoked climate change has occurred, forest fires have been documented at a rate well above that which is natural. This rate is one of the natural scientific indicators that climate change is occurring, and that human development has created an unstable environment.

Deforestation from development aside, the overwhelming factor contributing to climate change is the emission of carbon dioxide and other greenhouse gasses as a result of the burning of fossil fuels (Figure 5.2, for example). How are the majority of fossil fuels burned? Transportation: automobiles, trucks, busses, motorcycles, and industry: power plants, industrial manufacturers, resource extraction and refinement are all key components of greenhouse gas emissions. Car emissions are a key example of an exponential effect. The manufacturing plants that churn out cars are constantly polluting the atmosphere. Similarly, the power plant that provides electricity to the manufacturing plant, whether coal fired, nuclear or gas/oil also creates plenty of pollution. When a car is on the road it acts as a miniature version of those plants, producing similar pollutants from its exhaust pipe: carbon dioxide, sulphur nitrogen dioxide, etc.

Often associated with the concept of hybrid gas-electric, biodiesel, and specifically hydrogen fuel cell cars is the idea that their proliferation and technological perfection will neutralize the problem of greenhouse gas emissions. Let us use the example of a hydrogen fuel cell vehicle, hypothetically produced by Ford in Ontario. If such a vehicle where to be mass produced and used, replacing all the gas cars that Ford currently sells in Ontario, pollution would be reduced. This is because fuel cell cars use compressed hydrogen gas ($H2$) as fuel. When the hydrogen gas is exposed to the oxygen gas ($O2$) found naturally in the atmosphere, water is created along with a little spark of electricity. The water, a product of the reaction, is emitted from the tail pipe instead of the normal greenhouse gas fumes; the electric sparks from the reaction power the car. At this point of the process, no environmental damage is caused: the products of water and electricity are not pollutants. But what of the car's manufacture? In order to build the cars themselves, the Ford plant still relies on the coal or nuclear power that makes up a portion of Ontario's electrical output. Both the manufacturing and power plant still contribute pollution as a result of the car's existence. What is more: there is no natural form of isolated hydrogen gas. As stated above, resource extraction and refinement is another form of industry that contributes to pollution. To obtain the compressed gas fuel needed to power the car, hydrogen has to be isolated from water ($H2O$). To do this, an electric spark is needed to break the bond between the hydrogen and oxygen (the spark needed contains the same amount of electricity that results in the fusion of these two elements in the car's reaction)[91]. If the power that is used to create the isolating spark comes from a non renewable resource, such as coal, then again pollution results and the benefits of the hydrogen fuel cell is impinged. They are not eliminated however, as the method to refine gas that resides in current gas stations uses polluting coal and nuclear power as well. A hydrogen fuel cell or similar non-polluting car addresses the most superficial – though considerably weighty – level in the greenhouse gas equation; it would not rectify the situation. For clarity, the concept of the car's process is summarized below. The root of the problem, in the system of car production and use, is the method by which energy is initially harvested. If the system where to evolve so that the electricity that isolated the hydrogen fuel and powered the manufacturing plant was renewable and non-polluting and the cars themselves used the fuel in a non polluting reaction, then the entire system would be travelling towards sustainability: the problem would be solved in each, not just one, area. Such methods of producing electricity already exist.

Figure 5.3: Conceptualizing the Car

	Status Quo	Status Quo + Hydrogen Fuel Cell Cars	Completely renewable and sustainable system
Car Fuel Source	Gas: when burned for fuel produces GHG, pollution.	Compressed Hydrogen Gas: when used for fuel produces water, no GHG or pollution.	Compressed Hydrogen Gas: when used for fuel produces water, no GHG or pollution.
Refining Fuel	Usable gas is refined (by-products of refinement create pollution), using power from non renewable sources, produces pollution.	Hydrogen is isolated from water using power from non renewable sources, produces pollution.	Hydrogen is isolated from water using renewable sources: wind, solar, bio, small scale hydro, geothermal, tidal, no pollution.
Manufacturing Cars	Raw materials are extracted from earth (minimal use of recycled material) and processed into car, powered by non renewable resources: produces pollution.	Raw materials are extracted from earth (minimal use of recycled material) and processed into car powered by non renewable resources: produces pollution.	Raw materials are extracted from earth at a sustainable rate. Majority of raw materials used are recycled and processed into car using power from renewable resources, no pollution.
Power Plants, Sources of Energy	Coal, Oil, Gas: emit GHG. Nuclear power: produces lost lasting, life threatening toxic waste. Large scale hydro: affects ecosystems, threatens rivers, and lakes.	Coal, Oil, Gas: emit GHG. Nuclear power: produces lost lasting, life threatening toxic waste. Large scale hydro: affects ecosystems, threatens rivers, and lakes.	Wind, solar, bio, small scale hydro, geothermal, cogeneration, tidal, future innovations. Renewable: no pollution.

Is the problem scientific or societal?

Is environmental degradation a problem large enough to merit higher priority in Canada? Should Canadians care about plants and animals to the point of not driving certain cars? The perils of climate change and pollution in general have been characterized as vague, alarmist, and the solutions seem utopian as opposed to grounded in scientific rigour. Does Canada need to address the issue of creating a sustainable society?

If climate change continues at its current rate, Canadians can expect more of the following: catastrophic weather conditions such as hurricanes, forest fires, severe heat waves, an upheaval of seasonal patterns, and an increase in conditions and diseases like skin cancer, asthma, and heart and lung disease. It was climate change that created the conditions necessary for the agricultural revolution millennia ago. Similarly contemporary climate change affects the planet's ability to grow *any* crops at all. Can you imagine trying to support over 6 billion people without any agriculture? The end result of a neglected environment is clear, and so are the signs that point to its likelihood, the only variables nebulous are where the point of no return is, and how much more time society has until it is reached.

There are certain variables in the earth's ecosystems that can be used to asses the health of the environment. Indicators – such as polar ice cap melting, forest fire frequency or climactic disasters of high proportion – are usually characterized by sensitivity to adverse changes in the environment, such as global warming. Another example of such an indicator is found in the populations of amphibian species. The health of an amphibian population within an ecosystem is often the best indicator of the health and stability of that ecosystem as a whole. This is due to intrinsic qualities that all amphibians posses. Amphibians breathe air, and are therefore sensitive to polluted air. Amphibians also swim and most reside in water based ecosystems, making them sensitive to polluted water. Furthermore, amphibians have very thin skin that absorbs sunlight easily: making them sensitive to an environmental change such as an increase in UV radiation due to atmospheric ozone depletion. From these basic characteristics the reasons why amphibians are both the leading life form in extinction rate, and percentage of species endangered can be derived.

When it comes to sustainability, solutions are not as simple and problems solvable as the example of the car's fossil fuel infrastructure is in technological and engineering terms, as they are politically. Technological innovation often follows the rule of thumb: 'necessity is the mother of invention'. Why non sustainable systems – such as the automobile industry – remain in place, is easier to understand through the filter of economics and politics, as opposed to science. For example, Americans and Canadians are relatively spoiled (Figures 5.4 and 5.5) when it comes to gas prices and car selection, consumers and industry both being at fault. Let us look at what market factors have done to certain European states.

Figure 5.4: Retail Premium Gas Prices USD/Gallon (including Taxes)[92]

Date	Belgium	France	Germany	Italy	Netherlands	U.K.	U.S.
3/14/05	5.73	5.60	5.83	6.00	6.48	5.92	2.24

Despite substantially lower gas prices enjoyed in North America, the common portrayal of gas prices is that they are ludicrously high. Even if prices were to double: relative to other first world and G-8 countries it seems that the price of gas is very inexpensive, and that Canadians and Americans are not justified in complaining. Upon closer inspection of the fluctuation of gas prices in Canada over a 36 month period (Figure 5.5), one can begin to see why consumers are irate. Fluctuation in a commodity's price makes for an unstable personal monthly expenditure, and middle and lower class citizens who budget their monthly cheques seem to have little reasonable indicator of what the price of gas will be in a given month.

Figure 5.5[93]: Canadian prices (in US$/Gallon for comparison with 5.4)

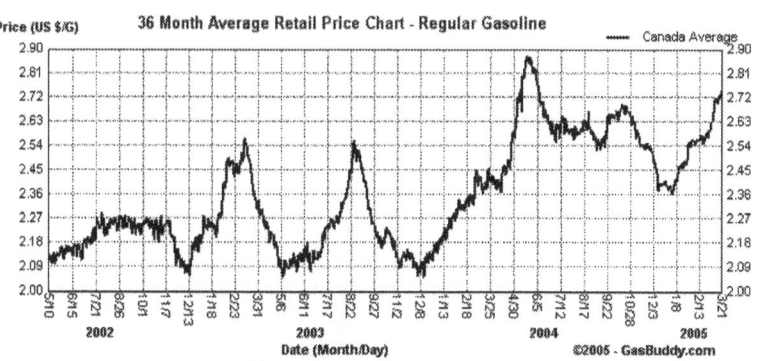

What causes such a high level of uncertainty? The Middle East is one of the most politically instable areas in the world, and it is also a large source of oil and gas resources. Through the NAFTA, Canadian gas prices are inextricably linked to those in the US. Political instability creates economic uncertainty; hence market factors that link directly to gas prices will fluctuate. For example, everyday since the United States occupation of Iraq began, the insurgent forces have been attacking the oil and gas infrastructure that makes the country such a valuable commodity to the West. The number of attacks has varied, but on a given day they outnumber those on civilian or military targets by a large margin. The US was aware that any resistance would focus on the oil infrastructure. After military victory was assured, US and British forces did not immediately secure the streets of Baghdad, and did not try to achieve order, law and peace. Instead they first secured the oil fields, refineries, and pipelines. The result was the looting that took place during the initial week of power vacuum. Memories of Saddam Hussein's fleeing Iraqi forces setting fire to the oil fields of Kuwait in 1991 compelled the United States to not do the right thing, they eventually moved to stop the looting and secure a (somewhat) higher level of order, but only after a good deal of chaos had ensued. The value in stabilizing the oil supply dictated their initial actions, and stability in supply, demand and price, perhaps more than actual price itself is important to American and Canadian companies and consumers. The battle to maintain stable lower gas prices goes far past economics and runs all the way to US military actions. Taking into account those costs associated with low gas prices in North America, dead Americans and Iraqis for example, that are currently not tabulated in the bottom line figure; one has to conclude that a more cost effective source of energy is available.

What dynamic has this disparity in gas prices created in the European markets versus those in North America? The US Census Bureau found that SUV registration increased by 81% between 1992 and 1997, followed by a 56% increase between 1997 and 2002[94]. While "SUVs account for only 5 percent of European vehicle sales, compared with 26 percent of the U.S. market."[95] Similar trends can be found in Canada, where the number of SUVs, Minivans, and Trucks on the road since 1990 has doubled, while the total number of cars has slightly decreased[96]. The disparity in the price of gasoline stymied growth of the SUV market in Europe at the same time it surged in North America. US companies like GM and Ford have had no problem producing larger, less efficient models, and neither have European companies like BMW and Mercedes-Benz, but they only sell them in North America. SUVs, Minivans and Trucks are naturally more expensive, and hence companies would rather sell and advertise them. The marketing of the SUV has driven consumer segments like suburbanites – who lack any necessity to own a gigantic vehicle – to buy SUVs in droves. Characterizations of SUVs in America are easy to come by: "In the United States, SUVs' size and stature appeal to Americans' romance with the open road and the endless horizon. Middle-class folks buy them to get a feeling of security in an insecure world."[97] In comparison

Swedes have taken to calling SUV drivers 'Montessori wagons or jeeps' and in England they are 'Chelsea tractors', alluding to the idea that rich urban or suburban people drive SUVs frivolously, in non hazardous driving conditions, such as to drop their children off at school.

Complete solutions to gas guzzling and other environmental problems that do not involve the capricious wax and wane of market factors may be impossible to implement in Canada. Because Canada has signed onto the NAFTA, involving the United States and Mexico, and is a member of the World Trade Organization (WTO), certain regulations could be illegal to pass into law. NAFTA, for reference came into force in 1993 (an updated version of the 1988 Free Trade Agreement), along with the WTO which was a modernization of the old General Agreement on Trade Tariffs (GATT 1948). Now those labelled as 'right-wing' economists, 'integrationists', and 'neo-liberalists' will say that these two bodies are essential to the progress of industry, the economy, and the workforce. That they saved Canada: from recession, escalating debt and inflation, and a loss of corporate investment and therefore jobs. Whether these agreements have spurred such results is not a moot point, but what is clear is that their implementation was concretely short-sighted when it came to environmental impact. Both the NAFTA and WTO strive to 'break down the barriers' that inhibit more production and trade. A barrier is often a euphemism for a tariff or fine placed on a country's imports, or a subsidy on commodities exported. Other times these agreements facilitate the deregulation of an industry or institute common regulations between states: "Standardizing some business regulations"[98] is a phrase often used. Paul Martin recently expanded and clarified the NAFTA in 2005, with the Security and Prosperity Partnership of North America agreement, whose goal was to make North American markets competitive with the markets of the European Union and China through said clarification. When a reporter asked about fears of economic integration leading to a decrease in Canadian sovereignty at the agreement's press conference in Waco, Texas, Martin spoke of the need for common regulations.

He proffered an example, the seat belt. The automobile industry is prevalent in all three countries in question, and therefore should have shared safety regulations. There is certain logic to this: if regulations on seat belt strength and safety are soft in Mexico, and Mexican made GM cars are imported to Canada while not meeting Canadian safety regulations, one of two problems could arise. The cars will probably be caught by Canada's regulatory net, and sent back to Mexico at a cost to the Mexican economy, the GM profit line, and ultimately the Canadian consumer (because with decreased choice a more expensive car market is likely). If that does not occur, the cars could simply be placed on the market anyway, and some Canadians may or may not die as a result (if the Canadian safety standard is well founded). As logical as the seat belt example may be, dangerous consequences lurk in examples other than seat belts; like shrimping gear, bovine growth hormones, and catalytic converters.

Small gas engines like those used in lawnmowers, snow blowers, weed wackers, snowmobiles, all terrain vehicles, and mopeds produce a lot of pollution in Canada. Larger gas engines like those in cars, trucks, and busses all produce less pollution, relative to their size, than small engines because of one basic attachment: the catalytic converter. At one time catalytic converters were not available for small gas engines, it was thought that they could not be engineered at such a scale. So while catalytic converters have become assumed regulation for large engines, small engines remain without them. However, 15 years ago, a catalytic converter was invented for small engines. Since that time the design has been refined to become an engineering and scientific reality. It was estimated in a 2005 report by the CBC's "The National" that the end cost to the consumer buying a lawnmower, snowblower, ATV, or similar small engine machine with a catalytic converter would be 15 dollars[99]. It has also been estimated that these largely unregulated small engine devices contribute nearly 10% of total carbon dioxide emissions in Canada.

Gas lawnmowers typically cost between 200 and 600 dollars, and business wouldn't want that price range to escalate to between 215 to 615 dollars: driving away consumers. The majority of cars cost anywhere from 10,000 to 30,000 dollars. How much does the inclusion of seat belts add to that total I wonder? What is troubling is that while seat belts are well established as directly contributing to human health by dramatic car crashes and fatalities, subtler smog and global warming is less sexy, making it hard for a politician who never took biology to discern the definitive health hazards. What else is troubling is that the government is afraid and may even be legally unable to regulate something like small gas engine catalytic converters because of the NAFTA and membership in the WTO. If foreign industry or another state argued, through either the NAFTA's Chapter 11, or the WTO that cutting pollution from small gas engines is an impediment to lubricating production, trade and profit, as opposed to protecting the fundamentals of citizen health, then the Canadian government could be found in legal breach of those international agreements in introducing regulations that made catalytic converters mandatory for certain products. Just as the panels of the WTO and NAFTA have ruled against the US tariffs on Canadian softwood lumber, they could easily rule that required catalytic converters impeded cross border trade by forcing American manufacturers into frivolous production and costs. Such a ruling does not need to take place to subdue Canadian policy makers from passing (or even thinking about) such legislation. Joel Bakan, UBC professor, and corporate law expert discusses this at length:

> On numerous occasions the organization [WTO] has required nations, under threat of punishing penalties, to change or repeal laws designed to protect environmental, consumer, or other public interests[100]. In one case, for example, a U.S. law that banned shrimp imports from producers that refused to use gear that protected sea turtles from being accidentally snared, was deemed to violate WTO standards[101]; in another case, an EU measure that banned production and imports of beef from cows treated with synthetic hormones was similarly treated[102]. The full extent of the WTO's impact cannot be gauged from its formal decisions alone, however. As is true of any set of legal standards, WTO rules exert their strongest influence through informal channels. Governments might self censor their behaviour to ensure that they comply with the rules-as the state of Maryland did when it scuttled a proposed law that would have barred it from buying products from companies doing business in Nigeria (while that country was under the rule of a cruel dictatorship) after warnings from the U.S. State Department that such a law could expose the United States to WTO challenge. Governments can also use WTO standards to pressure other governments to change their policies, threatening to initiate a WTO complaint if they refuse to do so – as the United States and Canada did to get the European Union to back off proposed regulations that would have banned the import of fur from animals caught in leg-hold traps and of cosmetics that had been tested on animals[103].[104]

The World Trade Organization is void of democracy, there are no means by which Canadian voters can affect its rules and decisions: it is largely controlled by trans-national corporate industry. Blind faith that market factors will create an economic space where the environment becomes a priority before ecological collapse is a pipedream. Even Pierre Pettigrew, a standard bearer of Canadian involvement in the NAFTA and WTO speaks in similar terms, "I must say that I do not believe that the economy, left to itself, would serve humanity well."[105] Corporations, especially publicly traded ones, are in their current forms to make profit; anything detracting from the bottom line is irrelevant. Eminent and Nobel Prize winning economist Milton Friedman does not believe corporate responsibility exists: "Asking a corporation to be socially responsible makes no more sense than asking a building to be."[106] Corporations act predictably because they are just actors within a system. It is the system that needs to be modified so that corporations are put in a position to succeed. In terms of economic growth and profits with respect to the environment: conflict between the two should be legislated in a way that it is not in a corporations own interests to degrade the environment.

One idea prevalent in the discussion of how to create such a system is the triple bottom line sometimes known as 'true cost' accounting. 'True cost' refers to the idea that all economic costs should be accounted for, that corporations should not be in the business of making others pay for something like smog produced by their factories. Robert F. Kennedy argues that the principle of true cost accounting is not even in conflict with that of free market capitalism:

> The federal environmental laws passed after Earth Day 1970 were meant to restore…the free-market economy by forcing polluters to internalize their costs the same way they internalize their profits. I don't even consider myself an environmentalist anymore. I think of myself as a free marketeer [sic] who goes out into the marketplace and catches the cheaters and forces them to begin paying the true costs of bringing their product to market.[107]

Under true cost accounting, in the example of the Yellowknife oil drilling and refinery complex beginning the chapter, the business that used the river as a heat sink and chemical dump would have to pay for the environmental damage it caused to the river and surrounding ecosystem in a magnitude that exceeded what it would cost that company to install a sustainable processes, for example that cooled equipment and fluids so that no heat sink would be required and that neutralized excess product chemicals, rendering them harmless, or safely transported them elsewhere for other commercial use. Such penalties would make it in the best interests of the company to engage in environmentally sustainable business practices. 'True cost' accounting yields some interesting results when applied to the current forms of energy Canada relies on. Thomas Homer Dixon, author of *The Ingenuity Gap*, points to a conclusion reached by the Winnipeg International Institute for Sustainable Development: "The full cost of producing electricity by burning coal is actually 50 percent higher than the current market cost."[108]

I recently interviewed the owner of a Canadian 'off the grid' wind farm company, who was looking to make it in Ontario. I asked him some standard questions, about his wind generator's capacity, how the technology has been coming with respect to conversion percentage, and cost effectiveness. What is interesting is that after asking a plethora of technical questions, of which I was assuming he would stumble upon at least one, I got a plethora of good answers. Wind power has become technically feasible and cost effective. It is true that the wind does not always blow. However there are methods to buffer such a characteristic by combining renewable sources, and storing excess electricity that is not immediately needed. Supplementing a wind farm with solar power and small scale hydro can mitigate down times. When the wind is blowing, the sun shining, or the water running, and electricity is not being used, then excess electricity created can be utilised to isolate hydrogen gas from water. This hydrogen can be stored for later use when more electricity is needed than immediately available. The problem with wind power breaking into Ontario markets off the grid is not even its cost effectiveness per se. Germany has the largest population of wind farms in the world, while benefiting from less wind than Ontario per year. If the electricity market was completely laissez faire in Ontario, wind turbines would be a competitive source of power in terms of *single bottom line* costs, competitive with coal, nuclear, and hydro. What is holding wind back in Ontario is not the technical feasibility of wind power. It is not even that the price of coal and nuclear power are not based on true multiple bottom line costs (which they flagrantly are not). It is that the single bottom line cost of electricity to the average Joe is not even the real cost: it is the cost after government subsidy. It seems that once again, as with gas prices, consumers in Canada, and Ontario specifically in this case are spoiled. In 2005, the average Ontarian paid 5 cents a kilowatt hour for electricity, with a paltry increase of .8 cents, to 5.8 for every kilowatt over 750 per month. In Germany citizens currently pay a minimum of 14 cents per kilowatt hour. The difference is not that Germany uses more expensive wind power, it still only makes up a small fraction of their total output; the difference is that the Ontario and Canadian governments subsidize the hydro, nuclear and coal power, driving down the prices. Now, the fact that wind power would be more competitive in a free market does not mean that deregulation of (in this case) Ontario's market is the solution. If anything, wind power should be subsidized a great deal *more* than unsustainable coal, nuclear and large scale hydro power. Subsidizing unsustainable power may make it more affordable to everyone, but it has the negative consequence of impairing positive change. Under true cost accounting: wind, solar, small scale hydro, geothermal, hydrogen fuel cell, and biodiesel power sources would be subsidized so that they have a competitive advantage over traditional coal, nuclear, and large scale hydro. An example of this idea in action can be found in Sweden, which has had large success in subsidizing biodiesel fuels for cars so that their price competitively undercuts that of gas. A large population of consumers now drives the greener biodiesel cars – the subsidy expedited the conversion to sustainability. The wind farm company owner, when asked if the problem was technological, a mix of economical and political or perhaps legal, the answer I received was "strictly political". If wind power is unreliable how does Denmark already manage to have it make up 16%[109] of total power generating capacity?

Canadian Policy

It is obvious that Canadian politicians, and therefore Canadian policy, are lagging. The federal government is at the back of the pack with the provincial governments of Ontario and Alberta; meanwhile some proactive leads taken by Quebec and British Columbia, while heartening, are not enough. Whether it is lobbying from companies like the CNA (Canadian Nuclear Association) clouding their vision, or an ideological incapacity to comprehend the idea of environmental sustainability, or true costs, the majority of Canadians politicians from 2000-2005 were rhetorical and misinformed. Canadian policy makers continually refuse to put both people and businesses in a position to succeed. It could be argued that the market factors in the Nordic countries that elevated gas prices have created a space where, out of economic necessity SUVs became less prevalent and mass transportation, alternative fuels, and energy efficiency became endorsed by government. When looking at those Nordic countries (plus Uruguay), it would seem that Canada is in a position to succeed based on two shared characteristics. The ESI report summarized "The five highest-ranking countries are Finland, Norway, Uruguay, Sweden, and Iceland – all countries that have substantial natural resource endowments and low population density."[110] Canada obviously has substantial natural resources, and a population density that is substantially lower than Sweden, Norway, Uruguay, and Finland, and is comparable to Iceland's[111]. Canada like Sweden, Norway, Iceland and Finland's also has a cold weather climate: something often cited as a reason holding Canada back from increasing environmental sustainability. The fact that a climate is cold will merely affect the details of sustainable solutions; it by no means exempts their possibility. In the cases of those Nordic countries' movement towards sustainable solutions, there are two factors: the will of individuals to make a positive change, and the ability of the government to put them in a position to succeed, that are missing in Canada.

Market factors focussing singularly on one bottom line do not take into account all the detrimental externalities resulting from bad environmental policies. The robotic economic thinking of the Paul Martins and Stephen Harpers – the prototypically successful Canadian politicians – are conducive to single bottom line thinking. Not only does neither believe in such things as true cost accounting, they do not believe in single bottom line mechanisms (i.e. market incentives) for protecting the environment. Why not provide market incentives to companies who move in the right direction? Tax breaks for companies that refit their buildings to be energy efficient, that reduce the pollution of factories and power plants, that invest research dollars in sustainable solutions, and sell environmentally progressive products are all examples of such market incentive policies. Current market incentives to conserve electricity are ridiculous. The increase in price from 5.0 to 5.8 cents per kilowatt hour after 750 kilowatt hours is a laughable deterrent to members of the population that can afford 30,000 dollar SUVs.

For example, there are merits to the idea of instituting regulations that make renewable and cost saving methods mandatory in house construction. Homes that are built with water heaters mainly powered by rooftop solar panels are both scientific reality and an economically profitable enterprise. As one will see later, that regulation alone could significantly reduce an individual's greenhouse gas emissions. It would also stimulate small business growth in creating a new market. If a business owner cuts his factory's electricity, gas, and water bills by 20% each through refitting his buildings, then he owes less in bills: contributing to his profit while lessening environmental impact. If a company pays less money on their electricity bill over a three year period than they invested in refitting their office they would not gripe about the regulation, it would be in their business interest. Typically, the biggest companies are the biggest polluters, the last thing a large business wants to do however, is hire more workers. What about a refitting program run by post-secondary education institutions that: upgrades building efficiency at a cost that is profitable to businesses, and employs people looking for work and experience with knowledge of construction and the environment. Canadian universities and colleges have great co-op programs that process a lot of students who need work, for a summer, or for a semester. This type of environmentally sustainable solution is a perfect example of how a Public-Private Partnership or P3 could be effective: it is profitable to the company, and is a good investment for the public. If the legal (and therefore economic) system places business in a position where making environmentally sustainable decisions is less profitable than making polluting decisions, then the legal system needs to be modified such that businesses are placed in a favourable position where decisions that positively affect profit, and positively affect the environment are synonymous. Apart from refitting programs, there are methods by which companies can produce their own power in sustainable ways from waste they already produce, and in ways that are profitable now, even under the censorship of a single bottom line economic system.

One of countless such examples can be found at Stelco Incorporated, Canada's largest steel manufacturer, based in Hamilton, Ontario. A healthy environment and energy efficiency is one of Stelco's stated goals: "Investing in improved energy efficiency and conservation in our operations and making every effort to use environmentally safe and sustainable energy sources to meet our needs."[112] Blast furnaces are a mainstay at a steel mill, and Stelco has two in continuous operation, one in Hamilton, and one in Nanticoke. The quintessential process in a blast furnace occurs in a vertical shaft where hot air and gas is released at the bottom (it then rises), and the ingredients in modern steel (coked coal, iron ore, and limestone) are released from the top of the shaft. These ingredients then meet the 'blast' on the way down, melting them and forming molten ore ready to be converted to steel. Old 'dirty' steel plants – such as the ones Stelco operates – merely let the hot air and gas escape after it rises through the shaft. However, a considerable amount of electricity was consumed creating that hot air and gas, and if it were harnessed after it had been used in the blast furnace process it could be converted back to electricity via a high pressure boiler (a modern steam engine). Tom Adams, director of Energy Probe, a non profit environmental think tank and electricity consumer advocacy group, told me that he conservatively estimates a minimum of 130 mega watts of baseline power could be harnessed using that method from the two blast furnaces alone: a significant reduction in demand for one company, compared to the 15000 to 25000 mega watts Ontario demands on average everyday. Since these furnaces run continuously, therefore so would the high pressure boilers, as well as the electricity being produced – or rather not being wasted. Making Stelco's process cleaner in this manner could easily be cost effective. Not only are the majority of new steel mills made with this technology incorporated, but Adams pointed out that previously 'dirty' mills similar to Stelco's – such as Mittal Steel's Ispat Inland Mill (3 blast furnaces) – have upgraded to this electricity conserving model in a profitable way. If this technical change to a steel plant is cost effective in a single bottom line marketplace, it leaves the only reason as to why Stelco has not made such a change a lack of business acumen. Perhaps another way of thinking about energy saving, environmentally friendly, and cost effective business regulations is that they are improving the baseline acumen of companies: they are making businesses work smarter.

From 1993 to as of this writing in 2005, the federal Liberal Party has compiled a dismal environmental record. After signing onto the Kyoto Protocol in 1998, they failed to implement a strategy to meet the commitments the agreement entails; hoping that Russia and the United States would not sign, resulting in a lack of ratification. Things were looking good when the Bush Administration announced they would rescind the United States' position of ratifying the Protocol in 2001. However Russia did finally sign on, albeit in 2004, meaning that Kyoto had exceeded the predetermined thresholds of 55% of all countries and 55% of total emitters needed for it to go into force. The Liberal plan backfired: instead of having the benefit of talking tough about the environment by signing Kyoto, while not actually having to significantly modify a budget or policy to meet Kyoto standards the Liberals put themselves in a position where their natal, non-comprehensive environment strategy had been exposed.

Since realizing they have to play catch up, the Liberals have feigned seriousness on Kyoto goals. The three main policy items since ratification have been: The One Tonne Challenge (March 2004), an agreement with Canadian Automakers (March 2005), and a Kyoto implementation plan (April 2005). All three of these policy items have already met their primary goals: press coverage of their release; and are good representations of the haphazard yet media savvy Liberal approach.

The One Tonne Challenge (OTC) is the government program that encourages individuals to reduce their GHG emissions, and it suffers from a few critical flaws. The first is evident in the opening line of the program's promotional website: "The One-Tonne Challenge *asks* you to reduce your annual greenhouse gas (GHG) emissions by one tonne. How? Use less energy. Conserve water and resources. Reduce waste."[113] (Emphasis added). Merely asking people to participate in a challenge is going to immediately wean out those who do not have time to volunteer and those who do not care about the environment. The second problem is that the program addresses the most superficial of levels in consumption. As polluting cars are the final product of a process that includes polluting car manufacturing plants, polluting mining and resource extraction: all powered by polluting electricity plants, people producing GHG are the final step in a similar process. Before going further, Figure 5.6 shows how each individual Canadian contributes in terms of GHG, for an average estimated total of five tonnes annually.

Figure 5.6: The average individual's GHG contribution[114]

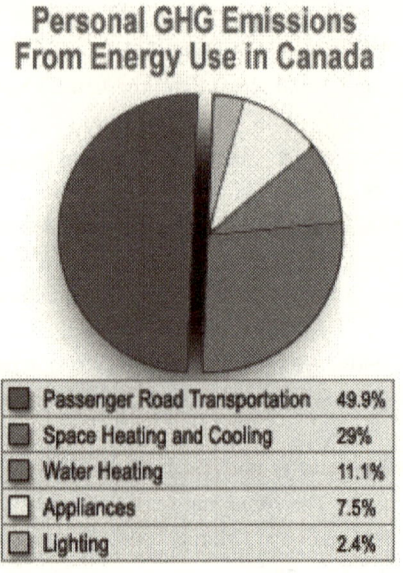

It is overwhelmingly obvious that the biggest factor in an individual's energy consumption is transportation. Space heating and cooling is also significant at 29%. Water heating, and appliance use and lighting also should not be ignored, combining for 21% of an individual's total energy consumption.

By being a voluntary program, the OTC is marketing towards the niche population of civic minded citizens who for the most part, probably already knew about climate change and energy conservation. The current incentives as described by the government, for an individual to take the challenge are "Save money/ Help fight climate change/ Improve our air quality/ Protect the environment"[115] If the federal government wants to be serious about meeting Kyoto commitments, an awareness that the only effective incentive of those four is 'saving money', might better sculpt strategy. As the current incentives to saving money are *demonstrably ineffective* the OTC is dependant solely on active participation. The monetary incentive for being conservative when it comes to an individual's transportation can be summarized in the cost of purchasing a vehicle and the cost of running it, i.e. gas prices. Since 1990, the total number of automobiles in Canada has decreased from 11.106 million to 10.867 million, while the number of less efficient (and therefore more gas costly) SUVs, Vans, and Trucks has increased from 3.256 million to 6.840 million[116]. Furthermore, this growth in larger vehicles has been unabated, increasing markedly every year. Not only do these larger vehicles cost more when first purchased, their remarkably poor fuel efficiency makes them considerably more expensive to run. Clearly, savings from more fuel efficient cars alone are not enough of an incentive for an individual to reduce their GHG emissions in the important transportation category.

The second half of GHG emissions attributed to individuals also lacks an effective conservation incentive. The main strategy to induce people to save on their bills is by following efficiency tips provided by OTC promotional material. Figure 5.6 shows Space Heating and Cooling, Water heating, Appliances, and Lighting: all consumption areas that can be paid for by an individual through their electricity bill (though some water heaters use gas etc), and which conserving power would therefore positively affect. How significant was the monetary incentive to conserve power in the year of the OTC's release? In the province thirstiest for electricity (therefore the most in need of conservation) the incentive is paltry. During the summer, the peak consumption season, of 2005 the subsidized price of electricity in Ontario was 5 cents per kilowatt hour, for the first 750 kilowatt hours of monthly use. After a household exceeded 750 kilowatt hours within that month, the price raised to 5.8 cents per kilowatt hour. The average household expenditure in Ontario is 1000 kilowatt hours per month[117], which can be substantially higher in the summer. Under the 5.0/5.8 price structure, 1000 kilowatt hours a month costs $52, while 2000 costs $110 (plus tax)[118]. If someone can afford a 30,000 dollar SUV, how much of an impact does a rate increase of .8 cents make?

Subsidizing anything, including electricity prices, means high income citizens will pay more of the cost than low income citizens. All things are equal when it comes to paying the final electricity bill with prices of 5.0 and 5.8 cents per kilowatt hour: how much electricity one used is directly proportional to what one pays. However, the money that was invested to create that subsidy (to lower it from the free market price) was collected in taxes. Since high income earners pay a bigger percentage of earnings in taxes, a high income individual ends up paying more for electricity than a low income individual: this is the goal of the subsidy, to redistribute the cost in the hierarchy of wealth so that everyone can afford what is seen to be a nearly essential commodity. With this in mind, coupled with the proven fact that there is a high income segment of the population that will not be affected by certain monetary incentives for want of luxury (i.e. suburban dwellers purchasing SUVs), is it a surprise that Ontario power consumption reached all time highs in 2005? Converse to high income counterparts, the group that is likely to be affected by incentives to conserve are low income earners. Why subsidize the price of electricity past the threshold of its essentiality? If high income earners are going to ignore their electricity bill because comparable to their income, it is insignificant, then why not have a price structure as follows: the first 250 kilowatt hours at 5 cents per hour, then between 250 and 1000 kilowatt hours at 8 cents an hour, and after 1000 kilowatt hours let the price be unsubsidized in the free market. This price would be the full price, and therefore able to fluctuate like gas prices. If high income earners are willing to purchase large vehicles at significantly higher prices than cars, and run them with significantly higher gas bills, then they will be willing to pay significantly higher electricity prices. Electricity is subsidized to make it affordable to all because it is defined as a necessity. Past an arguable point, perhaps 250 or 500 kilowatt hours per month, energy consumption no longer is a household necessity but a luxury, one that contributes significantly to climate change. Food is also seen as a necessity, and as a commodity is more valuable than electricity. The government funds food banks to provide free (i.e. subsidized to a price of zero) food for those who cannot afford it. What the government does not purposefully do however, and contrasting its policy on electricity, is drive down the price of McDonald's through subsidy in order to encourage rich citizens to become obese. Clearly, the current incentive structure is not strong enough to warrant any changes when it comes to luxurious power consumption.

Despite all the flaws in the OTC's approach, even if real conservation incentives existed, the program's success would only fix a segment of the problem. According to Environment Canada, the 5 tonnes of GHG each individual produces only makes up 28% of total GHG emissions annually[119] (it is closer to 21%). This leads to the second portion of the Liberal's seven-year-too-late Kyoto plan: their agreement with Canadian Automakers. The OTC set a goal of having each individual reduce their emissions from 5 tonnes to 4 tonnes per annum, a difference of 20%. Referencing Figure 5.1 the total emissions in 2002 were 731 Mt or approximately 20% above 1990 levels. The Kyoto Protocol commitments are actually 6% lower than 1990 levels, and from 2002-2005 emissions have increased substantially. This might lead one to conclude that the reductions necessary in a sector are actually somewhere between 25 and 30%. Despite these discrepancies, one would expect that the government would target a goal consistent with the 20% reduction sought by the OTC for all variables in the equation, including automakers for example: the idea of evenly diversified pressure. This was flagrantly not the case when the federal government made a non-binding agreement with Canadian automakers in March 2005.

According to Environment Canada's Greenhouse Gas Inventory, Road Transportation made up 137 Mt[120] of Canada's 731 Mt of GHG emissions in 2002 (this 137 Mt was a subtotal of the 190 Mt attributed to transportation as a whole: including aviation, rail, and marine emissions). In 2005, (as the 137Mt has surely increased in the three years since 2002) Canadian Automakers agreed in principle to reduce their emissions by 5.3 Mt, or 3.87% of the 137 Mt produced in 2002. "'I would say this is a deal of epic proportions,' auto consultant Dennis DesRosiers said."[121] Environment Minister Stéphane Dion claimed "I'm very pleased I will have the mega tonnes that I need for the Kyoto plan"[122] Taking into account that: a) there is no method the government has of enforcing the 5.3 Mt commitment: the deal is merely a handshake b) the trend of increasing SUV ownership and c) the fact that a 5.3 Mt commitment is only 3.87% of the conservatively calculated figure of 20% that is actually needed to meet Kyoto Protocol commitments, do you think that Stéphane Dion actually has the mega tonnes that he needs from the auto industry?

The third piece of the overdue plan was the release of "Project Green" – an updated version of the (more) abysmal 2002 Kyoto Plan: "Climate Change Plan for Canada" – and it followed the same trend that has characterized the Liberal approach. Of Project Green, Matthew Bramley of the Pembina Institute said, "Taxpayers are going to take on a stiff burden of cost to find emissions reductions for Kyoto while industry is really going to be asked to make what really represents an economically insignificant contribution." The One Tonne Challenge already tackles (albeit poorly) the most superficial plane of the problem, the root causes are industry and most specifically electricity generation: which are not adequately addressed in Project Green. In 2002, coal power generated about 18.8% of the total electricity in Canada (compared to 59.7% for Hydro, 12.3% Nuclear)[123]. However of the total GHG emissions from electricity generation, coal generated a vastly unproportional 80.3% of total GHG emissions[124]. Yet when it comes to shutting down coal plants in Canada, or investing heavily in mitigating this unproportionality, government is meek and lacks leadership. Not only does it seem like the lifespan of coal plants may be extended indefinitely, provincial governments have been unable to grasp the fact that the generational capacity lost will need to be replaced by new renewable sources. In Alberta there is such disregard for the idea of ending reliance on coal power that new coal plants are being built so their power can be exported to the United States. What are not directly exported in this process though, are the coal plants' GHG emissions.

New green business ventures spring up everyday, hoping their timing is right; anticipating they will catch the expected boom of consumer environmentalism. Meanwhile, old businesses such as General Motors, the decedents of Standard Oil, and British Petroleum put on a visage of environmental investment, window dressing for the public, while trying to maintain the status quo of the market. Sir John Browne, head of British Petroleum and an advocate of 'corporate responsibility', especially when it comes to green initiatives had this to say: "The days when our business had a captive market for oil are probably ending. There are new sources of supply in almost every part of the energy market. Even in transportation it is likely that advances in the technology of fuel cells will soon give us cars with different engines. So we have to compete to ensure that oil remains a fuel of choice."[125] This seems far removed from the ideas advertised by British Petroleum, or those associated with BP's environmentalist logo. For copyright reasons, the floral, green and yellow logo cannot be included in the book, but is plastered all over BP's website: <http://www.bp.com/home.do>. British Petroleum is an example of a company that portrays themselves as environmentally conscious while possessing fundamental characteristics that make it impossible for the company in the current marketplace to actually be so. Monolithic and antediluvian companies such as BP are not good for the economy or the environment, and are polar opposite to the type of business Canadian government should desire to thrive in the energy and transportation sectors: new small and green businesses. Small business growth is that coveted of economic indicators amongst governments for good reason. New, small, and independently owned businesses proportionally employ more people than larger, older, and publicly traded corporations, in addition to adding strength to the economy in diversified investment. The Canadian federal government's "Project Green" has not used this idea to foster green industry growth in anticipation of the emerging Canadian and global markets for sustainable development technologies. The federal government has remained a staunch subsidizer of big oil.

The Liberal Plan includes budgetary investment made into renewable energy research, and a plan for Large Final Emitters (LFE) to reduce their emissions. The term LFE encompasses companies in mining and manufacturing, oil and gas, and thermal or coal electricity: a collection that criss-crosses sectors such as industry and electricity, resource extraction and manufacturing having one thing in common, high GHG emissions. By the government's own calculations, the conglomeration of GHG sources that make up LFE is responsible for nearly 50% of total emissions[126]. One would therefore expect that if individuals were expected to reduce their emissions by 20%, then LFE would also face a similar target. Project Green calls for a 45 Mt reduction from LFE by 2010 – not from current levels however, like individuals are being asked to do – but from projected emission levels. 50% of the projected emissions in 2010, (Fig. 5.1) is 404.5 Mt. But 45Mt of 404.5Mt equates to 11.1% or 8.9% shy of what individuals are being asked to contribute and roughly 14-18% shy of what is estimated to be necessary to reach Kyoto goals. Even if the mechanisms by which the government imposed this reduction on industry were strong, which they are not[127], they would still be well short of meeting Kyoto goals in this sector if the program was an overwhelming success. Indeed, all three parts of the Liberal plan can be described as such: feeble incentives towards a goal that if reached will not result in fulfilling the actual commitment.

The worst part of the Liberal plan occurs when Kyoto commitments are not reached. Under the Protocol, countries that do not meet or do not want to meet, their standards can purchase emissions credits from other countries that have. Russia is one country that in all likelihood will easily meet its commitments, and hence have plenty of credits to spare. The Liberal party plans to make up the difference between the goal and the actual level achieved by purchasing emission credits from a country such as Russia; that is to say they are planning to not honour the commitment in advance. This is not a contingency plan that they will be forced to activate if Canada misses – it is part of the plan – and it makes no economic sense. Buying emissions credits from Russia while still polluting at home is similar to producing coal power in Alberta and selling it to the US, except in the case of emission credits, Canada is losing money (Alberta is gaining it), while still polluting its own air.

Perhaps even more important than the lack of fiscal diligence and principle that intentionally missing the commitments entail is the message it will send to the United States. In the period from 2005 to 2010 when the goals of Kyoto are undertaken, Canadian companies will be at a competitive disadvantage to American companies in the single bottom line marketplace of North America, even if companies do not have to cut back enough, and even if the only thing a company does is install GHG monitoring systems that it wouldn't have otherwise. The next phase of the Kyoto Protocol will occur in 2008-2012, and may well be the last chance to woo the United States, and other non Kyoto countries, such as Australia to join the agreement's membership. Japan, Canada, the United States and Australia all share a common marketplace and common characteristics. Japan and Canada ratified the

Kyoto Protocol, despite knowing that if the United States and Australia did not, they would most likely actively undermine the competitiveness of certain Japanese and Canadian companies. If Canada cannot be an exemplary state, by showing the United States and Australia that Kyoto commitments can a) actually be reached b) be done in a fiscally responsible way and c) be done in a way that spurs new industry and makes existing industry more efficient, strengthening the economy instead of hurting it, the chances either country will ratify the Kyoto Protocol in its second phase diminish exponentially. Under the Liberal plan as it currently stands, Canada will miss its goal of reducing GHG to 6 percent below 1990 levels by a sizable margin. Ratifying the Kyoto Protocol and going halfway (hence having to buy credits) makes less economic sense than either ratifying it and reaching the targets or not ratifying it at all. Not fulfilling this commitment will negatively affect the environment and the health of citizens, but also harm Canada's credibility, the future chances the United States will ratify Kyoto, and will hence disparage future international cooperation on the environment in general.

Priorities

The environment as a societal issue is instructive. Environmental investment can be an economic efficiency stimulator, from refitting programs and smart green regulations, to encouraging the creation of small businesses. Environmental health can struggle against the measurements of economic growth or can be synonymous with its progress. Types of environmental degradation, through global warming for example, provide insight into exponential effects. Global warming not only increases the temperature of the earth in an accelerating fashion, it catalyzes more extreme weather conditions. The European heat wave of 2004 is an often cited example. Even Project Green acknowledges this idea and cites "events such as the BC forest fires (2003), the Prairie drought (2004)".[128]

Why a sustainable environment is not a higher priority is easy to see. With the current legal, economic and political structures in place, it is less than ideal for governments and businesses to either directly invest in environmental solutions to pollution, or to indirectly invest in environmental solutions by not polluting. Even those solutions that are cost effective in the current system – i.e. Stelco's high pressure boilers, or refitting for energy efficiency – are seldom seized upon: mainstream paradigm consists of the notion that only environmentalists care and should care about the environment, that environmentalism is anathema to business. The environment so obviously affects everyone, yet industry continues to lobby against environmentally smart regulation, and political parties continue to perpetuate their minimization.

Placing energy sources and technological design in the context of sustainability, it becomes apparent what is moving in the necessary direction and what is not. The end goal is sustainability, and hence renewable energy sources are the aptly named target. Renewable energy sources include, but are not limited to wind, solar, tidal, hydrogen fuel cell, geothermic, small scale hydro and various forms of biodiesel and cogenerated power. Just as these forms of power have emerged, future technologies have potential for different types of renewables. It is clear that nuclear energy and coal in their current forms (e.g. fission that produces hazardous waste versus unattained cold fusion) are inadvisable diversions from sustainability.

The fact is scientific sustainable solutions are everywhere, not limited to things like catalytic converters in small engines. Implementation of a hydrogen transportation infrastructure and a hydrogen energy economy are rooted in scientific rigour. New and viable renewable energy sources emerge every passing year. There are scientific solutions to factory farming, to fossil fuel use, to landfilling, to deforestation, and to climate change. The fact that there are technical solutions is not really what is in question when one comes to the point of making conclusions. Environmental sustainability is not a scientific problem, it is society's problem. The battle over investing in the environment has become between citizen groups. The influence of NGOs like Greenpeace, PETA, and the World Wildlife Fund seem to grow steadily everyday as networks of people from around the world join their causes. Even if corporate green investment is a large ruse to bolster market friendly images, what has resulted? Hybrid vehicles are more prevalent on the roads everyday and the GM Hy-Wire (a vehicle that actually runs on hydrogen) is an exceptional feat of engineering. Canada has entrepreneurial citizens, who care about their health. Canada enjoys a first world infrastructure, and an educated population with a plethora of universities, as well as a population that represents the world's assets. There is no reason that Canada cannot choose to be a leader in the world market in creating an environmentally sustainable economy and infrastructure. The most important group in this battle is not the NGOs, the corporations old or new, the governments, the power sectors, or the universities. The most important group is the individual citizen. The average individual citizen needs to recognize the urgency to move forward and the opportunity to create win-win dynamics in Canada. If the majority of citizens desire: to reduce pollution and nourish the environment (and therefore their health), to save power (and hence money), and in doing so create a market for Canadian environmental solutions, then the other groups listed will arrange themselves in step with these priorities. Everyone will realize that they have an interest in being 'environmentalists'. The results are clear: the public's motivation in Sweden and Iceland to be environmentally proactive prompted the government to act in that manner. Quebec's public opinion is slightly more open to sustainability than Ontario's, and hence some real solutions have been implemented in Quebec while Ontario flip flops.[129] If Canadian public opinion moves in a positive direction, one that understands more than just the health of trees are at stake, then the dominant institutions will follow: if Canada emulates the United States' complacent and blind eye approach, then the next generation of Canadians will be left with a much larger problem. The fact that the direction in which Canada moves depends on the motivation of its citizens could be said of many of Canada's issues, and illuminates who truly holds the power in society.

The environment was not always a political issue; it was previously seen in Western culture as treasure to be had and resources to be harvested. Through technology and industrialization, development and human expansion, the health of the planet has become increasingly important. The environment therefore provides an illustrative example of how new problems can arise from both progress in general and more specifically new technology: further reinforcing the idea that technology is not inherently good, but whose benefits or exploitations depend upon people themselves. Furthermore it questions our measurements of progress, that not all economic growth is desirable growth. The environmental struggle for sustainability also makes transparent where power lies in society today, and where the majority of it was centralized in the 20th Century, both in Canada, and on the international stage. Fossil fuel companies, from Imperial oil to British Petroleum and Royal Dutch Shell have had huge impact upon society and on the international geo-political landscape. Governments and government policy has reflected this power with the importance placed upon the fuel and energy markets. The opposition that environmental groups and activists have faced, the hurdles they have had to overcome displays how sheer capital, as opposed to reason, can make a politician's decisions for them. The idea that military power is no longer the dominant influence in the world, but economies and markets are, supports this. Finally, the environment displays the degree to which citizens are interconnected: how no person, whether Albertan oil baron, Ontario nuclear plant owner, Canadian politician or new born child is immune to a deteriorating environment and how no issue, whether health care, education or international trade is unrelated and unaffected by the condition of the natural world. In continuing societal progress, both in the world and specifically in Canada, the environment must be prioritized. Those who currently think they cannot afford to have the environment placed upon a pedestal should be encouraged by the idea that they can be put in a position to succeed by the system; whether they are energy corporations or middle class consumers, nuclear plant lobbyists, or environmental activists. The dangers of a deteriorating environment are clear, precise and definable as evidence by environmentally sensitive variables: the polar ice caps are melting, amphibians, the most environmentally sensitive species suffers from the highest rate of extinction, and in the past eight hundred years the world's forest coverage was nearly cut in half.

The most important idea to combat the notion that the environmental drive to sustainability is fruitless is: sustainability is not an endpoint to development, technology, or progress: sustainability is not an asymptote that cannot be reached. Sustainability is a precise and definable goal that, if achieved, would merely be a new benchmark, a starting point for new development and progress. Canada has all the characteristics requisite to lead. To reach this benchmark, this beginning of sustainable progress, paradigms must be shifted: sustainable design must change from option to postulate. People must be put in a position to succeed, by being informed, and by never being placed in a position to choose between livelihood and environment. Governments must be put in a position to succeed by being elected based on their environmental stance and record (perhaps such accountability could be found through electoral reform). Business must be put in a position to succeed by the law, so the goals of economy and environment are one. Everyone has to come to understand that the more biodiversity, the better off humans are, that a clean atmosphere and a vibrant population of duck-billed platypuses, while not obviously so, is in everyone's best interests.

Conclusion
What is the future of Canada?

"It is difficult to imagine that social coherence could be preserved decade after decade with economic growth occurring at the top of the prosperity pyramid and population growth at the bottom."
      – John D. Steinbruner in *Principles of Global Security*

"We can't solve problems by using the same kind of thinking we used when we created them."
      – Albert Einstein

Thus far I have issued many prescriptions. These prescriptions may be unique in their content and combination because of a variety of factors, not least that they were written while I was under twenty years of age. Youth favour solutions that employ the 'art of the possible': youth have not been entrenched in a status quo. Youth tend not to view solutions in terms of benefiting some and disenfranchising others. The only thing youth have a real interest in is the future. Hence youth favour long term thinking.

As an aside I do not think that youth today are disengaged in politics or citizenship in general. Voter turnout is low because some youth are apathetic yes, but the majority who do not vote are disillusioned. There is a great degree of civic activity among Canadian youth in terms other than voting, mainly activism and voluntarism. I have seen this first hand. I would caution those spending an inordinate amount of time worrying about the next generation's civic arousal, vis-à-vis the crumbling of Canada's democracy, that they are wasting their time. If voting is not perceived as an effective means, youth will not employ it.

I have argued that no national identity is necessary in Canada. When measuring a country's success, in what condition people live should take precedent over uniformity in self description. It seems to me that certain things, such as the division of people, or the conditions under which youth are voluntarily sent to their death in the name of defending or expanding arbitrary borders, are only possible with nationalism. While other things, such as a good health care system, good governance, a prosperous economy, and a sustainable environment are possible without nationalism. I have argued that a state is limited by the system with which it elects those who make decisions. Decisions on nationalism. Decisions on sustainability. Decisions on war. If the system by which citizens elect the decision makers is impaired, then decisions will be similarly impaired. I have argued that tradition and technology are not inherently good or evil, that their proliferation does not determine progress. I have warned against complacency in comfortable circumstances when compared to the circumstances of the past, or of others. I have argued that the life of a human is worth the same wherever that human was born and that any state's foreign policy must acknowledge this. I have argued that any decisions must understand the concept of exemplary action. I have similarly argued that Canada's relationship with the United States does not merit exception from such rules. I have argued that sustainability must change from option to postulate. That sustainability must become a tenet of society similar to the rule of law. That a social contract expiring with the exhaustion of resources needs rewriting.

In one sense, the entire book so far has been filled with case studies of how I think Canada should be. What have all these case studies told us?

Aristotle had two terms that described systems of government that were ruled by the people, that is, where the citizens of a state made the decisions. The first, polity, described a system of government where citizens made decisions based on the best interests of the community as a whole. The second, democracy, described a system where citizens made decisions based on what was best for them individually. The question posed in the title implies that Canada is either benefiting from the injustices of the current system while simultaneously and falsely advocating positive change; or that Canada is at the forefront of correcting injustice. Through the chapters it seems to me the more one knows the more one realizes that what is in the best interest of another is also in one's own best interest, and vice-versa. That when ignorance is dispelled: one realizes helping others is in one's own interest. When knowledge is gained, one concludes that shared prosperity is more sustainable and more profitable than prosperity garnered from inequitable oppression. *And so perhaps when fully formed understanding emerges, a citizen's prescription for the actions of the state does not depend on whether that citizen believes they live in a polity or a democracy.* Those in power, Canadians included, may believe that the self imposed nationalist divide between citizens, the inequality of the electoral system, the residues of past oppression, the domestic separation between the rich and the poor, the current inequity between the first and the third world, and the degradation of the environment for nothing but profit serves their best interest. That these things are necessary conditions for their comfortable positions in life, and that at the same time they need to appear to be fighting the very existence of such conditions in order to maintain such comfort. It is not just that the ideas have not reached our minds, or the knowledge has not permeated our brains. It is that those living in relative comfort are afraid, afraid of challenging the assumption that humanity is a zero sum game: that in all systems some will benefit and others will not. This does not have to be the case. Canada is not the leader in new progress. But by looking at those things that afflict this country, a case for true progress emerges. That perhaps oppression – systems designed for zero sum struggles – is not optimal. The belief that such exploitation is the least of all evils is a ruse.

Perhaps the future of Canada involves two possibilities. One involves following the same path, fooling ourselves that we are truly benefiting from the system, that the wolf's inordinate feast on the flesh of sheep will never come back to haunt us. As long as we remain in the wolf pack. As long as the sheep don't run out. The other path involves dispelling the ruse.

Endnotes

Those sources appearing in the endnotes are merely the ones cited, not a comprehensive list of all the literature and media that went into my research for this book. I have forgone a longer list of suggested further readings because of financial concerns, for that I apologize. That noted, these sources are a good start for those interested in further reading. For a further list of literature and information readers can contact me through this book's website on Trafford publishing's website. Most of the sources I have tried to make accessible to the reader: I have tried to include everything I can on the internet when given a choice. Internet and media resources should not be taken lightly as the ideas conveyed in these sources were as important as those in literature. It is also worth noting that a substantial amount of internet sources can be found in print, which is the case of most newspaper articles, archived news releases, government statements of expenditures, environmental and scientific reports, election figures, and speech transcripts. For internet news articles I used CBC news archive whenever possible due to its free nature and the generally long time articles remain in their online archive. Most New York Times articles are available online in archive with free registration, though some that are now in archive might be restricted. Those from the Globe and Mail, Toronto Star, or other publications may be not be universally available through the internet. In certain cases, I have tried to cite a proxy site for such unavailable archived articles, like Knight Ridder for example. A few hard copy sources, namely books may be available at certain libraries; however more recently published ones may not, an unavoidable fact for which I apologize to the reader interested in further discussion.

1   Klein, Naomi. "Boats, not Birthrights." *Great Questions of Canada.* Ed. Rudyard Griffiths. Toronto: Stoddard Publishing, 2000. 36.

2   Ornstein, Michael, and H. Michael Stevenson. *Politics and Ideology in Canada: Elite and Public Opinion in the Transformation of a Welfare State.* Montreal: McGill-Queen's University Press, 1999.

3   "The Aftermath." *Veteran Affairs Canada.* 2004. Veteran Affairs Canada. 6 Feb. 2005

    <http://www.vac-acc.gc.ca/remembers/sub.cfm?source=history/firstwar/canada/Canada19>.

4   Initially in Canada only women who had a relative or husband in the military gained suffrage.

5   "D-Day: Canada's role." *Canadian Broadcasting Corporation.* June 5, 2003. Robin Rowland. 10 Feb. 2005 <http://www.cbc.ca/news/dday/>.

6   "The 'who, what, when and where' of gender pay differentials." *Statistics Canada.* 19 June. 2002. Statistics Canada. 25 Jan. 2005 <http://www.statcan.ca/Daily/English/020619/d020619b.htm>.

7   Klein, Naomi. "Boats, not Birthrights." *Great Questions of Canada.* Ed. Rudyard Griffiths. Toronto: Stoddard Publishing, 2000. 44.

8   Hurtig, Mel. *The Vanishing Country: is it too late to save Canada?* Toronto: McClelland & Stewart, 2002.

9   Cooper, Robert. *The Breaking of Nations: Order and Chaos in the Twenty-First Century.* Toronto: McLellan & Stewart, 2003, 2004.

10   Griffiths, Rudyard. "Introduction" *Great Questions of Canada.* Ed. Rudyard Griffiths. Toronto: Stoddard Publishing, 2000. ix.

11   McLean, Rob, and John Godfrey. *The Canada We want.* Toronto: Stoddard Publishing, 1999.

12   Griffiths, Rudyard. "Introduction" *Great Questions of Canada.* Ed. Rudyard Griffiths. Toronto: Stoddard Publishing, 2000. xi.

13   Black, Conrad. *A life in progress.* Toronto: Key Porter Books, 1993.

14   Bissoondath, Neil. "Dreaming of Other Lands" *Great Questions of Canada.* Ed. Rudyard Griffiths. Toronto: Stoddard Publishing, 2000. 30-31.

15   Pettigrew, Pierre S. *The New Politics of Confidence.* Trans. Phyllis Aronoff and Howard Scott. Toronto: Stoddard Publishing, 1999.

16   Day, Stockwell. *LAW, DEMOCRACY AND HUMAN RIGHTS IN CANADA.* Harvard University, Boston. 28 Feb. 2005.

        Transcript available at: "Law Democracy and Human Rights in Canada." *STOCKWELLDAY.COM.* Feb 28. 2005. Stockwell Day. 5 March 2005 <http://www.stockwellday.com/feb2805.htm>.

17   Video available at: <http://www.cbc.ca/canadavotes/thecampaign/debate1.html>.

18   Which they are not. Stephen Harper never said he would take away "a woman's right to choose": he did want Canada to participate in the US invasion of Iraq, and he said he would invest in offensive military

strength including tanks and aircraft carriers. The Liberals were correct in declaring the second two, incorrect in the first.

19   Zinn, Howard. *Passionate Declarations.* New York: HarperCollins Publishers, 1990, 2003.

20   All election results unless are otherwise noted from: "2004 Federal Election Results". *Elections Canada.* 2004. 10 Feb. 2005 <http://www. elections.ca/scripts/OVR2004/default.html>.

21   Milner, Henry. "Political Drop Outs and Electoral System Reform." *Steps towards making every Vote Count: Electoral Reform in Canada and its Provinces.* Ed. Henry Milner. Toronto: Broadview Press, 2004. 23.

22   Doris Anderson, "PR would have saved the PCs." *Globe and Mail* 2 January 2004: A11.

23   "Canadian federal election, 2004." *Wikipedia, the free encyclopedia.* 2004. Wikipedia. 14 Feb. 2005, <http://en.wikipedia. org/wiki/2004_Canadian_election>.

24   50% would be the lowest percentage of riding seats that probably would be feasible in Canada as well as being considered ideal. Utilising a higher percentage of seats, say 75%, may have the effect of rendering a large party, like the Liberals for example, no list seats. This would also mean that the chances of a large party gaining more seats than they should are high. Another of the advantages of a list would be that if a party has perhaps 15 % of the popular vote in a province, but wins no riding seats, they could then assign a few of their list seats to be the unofficial representative, or caucus head, of that provinces portfolio. The smaller the percent of list seats, the better the chance that even with compensation the results will not be proportional. Also similar in affecting whether or not proportionality is achieved is not just the percent of compensatory list seats, but also the jurisdiction size within which they are assigned. The example simulation has that size within provinces. However, if they were assigned on a federal basis there would be greater flexibility in their application, resulting in a closer proportionality.

25   There are other variations upon this idea, one which includes casting one vote per person, that vote going to the candidate but also the candidate's party. A one vote system could work like this: If they voted for a party who was running a candidate in their riding, then their vote would go to that candidate, and also to the total of the party. If they voted for a party without a candidate in that riding, then their vote would simply go to that party.

26   There are two forms of lists, closed and open. Both would still have all the party's candidates on the list for public viewing at the start of a campaign. However, in a closed list system, the list that the party publishes would not be malleable, the order of candidate would be regardless of votes i.e. 1 Paul Martin 2 Anne McLellan... However, an open list system would allow for voters to rank which list candidates they liked and could yield 'list hopping'. So for example if Anne McLellan received more preferential votes than Paul Martin, she could 'hop' him and take the first Liberal list seat. Considering that there are 308 seats currently in Canada, and therefore the potential for 154 list seats or more, it seems unreasonable to ask voters to rank candidates in preference from 1 to 154 or 1 to 175. What seems more likely is that closed lists that have an inordinate amount of men near the top, or who have unpopular candidates near the top due to internal politicking would be punished by public opinion for placing unpopular candidates near the top of the lists, and this would be reflected in the garnering of their votes. This idea highlights the importance of making the lists public when the writ drops. A further complication of MMP in terms of the make up of the list is whether candidates who run are running in ridings can appear on the lists. This has yielded some interesting possibilities. Firstly, if they were allowed to be both on lists and in ridings, then high level candidates would have a greater level of security. However, a party, like the Liberal party, would not necessarily want to have Paul Martin as their number 1 list candidate and not run him in a riding if he could not do both. This is because if the Liberal party wins a hugely unproportional amount of seats through ridings, and that level is over their proportionality, even without any compensatory list seats, then Paul Martin would not be in the House. For example, using the 20 seat Conservative Liberal example with the addition of the NDP: if the Liberals won eight of the ten riding seats with 40% support in each of those eight ridings, compared to 35% in each riding of the conservatives and 25% in each riding of the NDP, then proportionally, the Liberals would only be entitled to those 8 seats. If the Conservatives won the other 2 riding seats, and had 35% of the vote they would be entitled to another 5 seats, to make 7 total. Finally, the NDP would be entitled to 5 list seats. In this case, the Liberals would receive no list seats, and therefore even the #1 candidate on their list would not be in the house. This should be tempered by the idea that party's can run their leader's in ridings that they are the most likely to succeed in, and are therefore safe from potentially not being in the house. It is hard to say whether or not having candidates on both slates in Canada would be a large problem, though a candidate's having two shots of success

would probably engender resentment amongst voters. If a riding based candidate was elected in their riding, then they would be skipped over in the list, because they would not be elected twice.

27 "Why is Turnout Higher in Some Countries than in Others?" *Elections Canada*. March 2003. Blais, André, Agnieszka Dobrzynska and Louis Massicotte. 20 Feb. 2005 <http://www.elections.ca/content.asp?secti on=loi&document=macro&dir=tur/tuh&lang=e&anchor=system&tex tonly=false#system>.

The conclusion that voter turnout is around 7 percent higher in countries with proportional systems can be found in: Blais, Andre and Ken R. Carty. "Does proportional representation foster voter turnout?" *European Journal of Political Research* 18 (1990): 167-82.

28 The story of the Bill that had trouble getting through in 1987 is an interesting one. At the time Brian Mulroney was trying to pass the GST bill, and pushed it through the House of Commons on the strength of his majority government. The Liberal dominated Senate however, did not pass the contentious Bill. However, there is a clause in Section 26 of the 1867 Constitution Act that gives in times of great stress or emergency, the Prime Minister the power to enlarge the size of the Senate temporarily for the purposes of passing a Bill. Brian Mulroney quickly invoked the clause, adding 8 more Senators to tip the chamber in the PC's favour. Upon the next vote the Bill passed.

29 "Statement of Expenditures." *The Senate Administration*. 2002. 8 Feb. 2005 <http://www.parl.gc.ca/information/about/process/senate/annualrep/0102/chapter6-e.htm>

30 "Census 2001." *Statistics Canada*. 2002. 7 Feb. 2005 <http://www12.statcan.ca/english/census01/products/standard/popdwell/Table-PR.cfm>.

31 "Senate Chambers throughout the World. How does Canada's Senate compare with other countries?" University of Lethbridge. January 8th 2004. Rhonda Lauret Parkinson. 24 Feb. 2005 <http://www.mapleleafweb.com/features/parliament/senate/senate-world.html>.

32 There are a variety of ideas on how to allocate seat winners based on preferential ballots. If there was a larger Senate size per province, ten for example, then voters could rank their selections from one to ten. They would not be compelled to rank them from one to ten, one to five or simply one would also suffice if they supported only five or one candidates.

33 This is a little far fetched, and would assume that Senators would not vote along party lines but rather provincial lines. However, if Canada is

to have a democratically elected Senate then there will be more power in Senators hands and hence more risk. Therefore the need to prepare for such a possibility is prudent.

34   "2000 Federal Election Results." *Elections Canada.* 2000. 29 Jan. 2005

< h t t p : / / w w w . e l e c t i o n s . c a / c o n t e n t . asp?section=gen&document=synopsis06&dir=rep/ 37g&lang=e&textonly=false>.

35   The model is based on Henry Milner's suggestion for Canada based on the MMP system adopted by New Zealand, not the MMP system adopted by Germany post WWII. Assumptions include a 5% minimum threshold for parties to gain compensatory list seats, or a victory in one riding seat. The ridings to list seat ratio is 50/50. The largest remainder-Droop formula was utilized in calculating overall results.

36   Jansen, Harold J. and Alan Siaroff. "Regionalism and Party Systems: Evaluating Proposals to Reform Canada's Electoral System" *Steps towards making every Vote Count: Electoral Reform in Canada and its Provinces.* Ed. Henry Milner. Toronto: Broadview Press, 2004. 50.

37   Johnson, William. *Stephen Harper and the Future of Canada.* Toronto: Douglas Gibson Books, 2005.

38   "The Christian Heritage Party of Canada." *The Christian Heritage Party.* 2005. The Christian Heritage Party. 9 Feb. 2005 <http://www. chp.ca/>.

39   *Canadian Charter of Rights and Freedoms.* Department of Justice Canada. 14 Feb 2005. <http://laws.justice.gc.ca/en/charter/>.

40   "What is the CHP in a nutshell?" *About the CHP.* 2005. The Christian Heritage Party. 9 Feb. 2005 <http://www.chp.ca/aboutTheCHP/>.

41   Caven, William. *The Equal Rights Movement.* Toronto: University Quarterly review, 1. 1890, 139-45.

H.D. Forbes, Ed. 1985. *Canadian Political Thought.* University of Toronto Press.

42   Ibid

43   Ibid

44   "Research scientists who work in public institutions often are troubled by the concept of intellectual property because their norms tell them that science will advance more rapidly if researchers enjoy free access to knowledge. By contrast, the law of intellectual property rests on

an assumption that, without exclusive rights, no one will be willing to invest in research and development (R&D)." Quote care of: "The Human Genome Project Information Page." *US National Library Online.* 2004. 20 Feb. 2005 <http://www.ornl.gov/sci/techresources/Human_Genome/elsi/patents.shtml>.

45   "2nd Bush-Kerry debate: Washington University, St-Louis Missouri." 8 Oct. 2004. *Commission on Presidential Debates.* 19 Feb. 2005 <http://www.debates.org/pages/trans2004c.html>.

46   Cooper, Robert. *The Breaking of Nations: Order and Chaos in the Twenty-First Century.* Toronto: First McLellan & Stewart, 2003, 2004.

47   Canada25's report: Eaves, David, et al. *From Middle to Model Power: Recharging Canada's Role in the World.* Toronto: Canada25. 2004. Ebook available at: <http://www.canada25.com/downloadreport.html>.

48   Bissoondath, Neil. "Dreaming of Other Lands" *Great Questions of Canada.* Ed. Rudyard Griffiths. Toronto: Stoddard Publishing, 2000. 30-31.

49   Zinn, Howard. *Passionate Declarations.* Boston: HarperCollins Publishers, 1990, 2003.

50   This was not always the case and there are ideas as to why this has happened. One explanation for this transformation is the "CNN effect". The idea being that people care about 'foreigners' or humanize people who live in other countries more easily because they can see them, and their struggles on TV, for example starving Ethiopian youth. Indeed domestic and foreign are polar opposites in meaning. But should domestic policy and foreign policy have different goals? It seems so obvious in retrospect that they should not. Are the people of Nicaragua so much different than the people of Canada? Are they worth less? If they are worth less than a different goal in policy is certainly justified. If they are worth less than a goal of domestic policy for all Canadians to be healthy and disease free, while having a foreign policy goal that is actively negligent of the health of Nicaraguans makes sense. If it is true that all people, regardless of citizenship, or assignment to a country, or residence in imaginary geographical lines are equal however, then the goals of foreign and domestic policy should in principle be the same.

51   "Canada in the World: Canadian foreign Policy review

1995" Foreign Affairs Canada. <http://www.dfait-maeci. gc.ca/foreign_policy/cnd-world/menu-en.asp>.

52   Bellamy, Alex J, Griffin, Stuart, and Williams, Paul. *Understanding Peacekeeping.* Cambridge: Polity Press, 2004.

53   "The problem is most critical in Africa, where up to 100,000 children, some as young as nine, were estimated to be involved in armed conflict in mid 2004. Children are also used as soldiers in various Asian countries and in parts of Latin America, Europe and the Middle East." Taken from: "Some Facts". The Coalition to Stop the Use of Child Soldiers. 2004. *The Coalition to Stop the Use of Child Soldiers.* 5 Feb 2005. <http://www.child-soldiers.org/childsoldiers/some-facts>.

54   "Canada's Foreign Aid." The Senate of Canada. 2003. *The Senate of Canada.* 30 January 2005. <http://www.sen.parl.gc.ca/lpearson/htmfiles/hill/26_htm_files/v26-Foreign_Aid.htm>.

55   OECD, Development Co-operation, 2003 Report, Paris, 2004. Also available at: "Canada's Foreign Aid." The Senate of Canada. 2003. The Senate of Canada. 30 January 2005. <http://www.sen.parl.gc.ca/lpearson/htmfiles/hill/26_htm_files/v26-Foreign_Aid.htm>.

56   Aleš Bulⵉ and A. Javier Hamann. The International Monetary Fund. February 2005. Volatility of Development Aid: From the Frying Pan into the Fire? The International Monetary Fund. 12 Mar 2005. <http:// www.imf.org/external/np/seminars/eng/2005/famm/pdf/hamann. pdf>.

57   "Canada's International Policy Statement". *Foreign Affairs Canada.* April 2004. Foreign Affairs Canada. 10 Feb 2005. <www.international.gc.ca>.

58   Love, Brian. "Fair trade tests G8 Goodwill on Africa." Reuters. July 10th, 2005.

59   "The Aftermath." Veteran Affairs Canada. 2004. Veteran Affairs Canada. 6 Feb. 2005

<http://www.vac-acc.gc.ca/remembers/sub.cfm?source=history/ firstwar/canada/Canada19>. "D-Day: Canada's role." Canadian Broadcasting Corporation. June 5, 2003. Robin Rowland. 10 Feb. 2005 <http://www.cbc.ca/news/dday/>.

60   Who were in favour of sending Canadian troops to Iraq to participate in the invasion and occupation. In fact they wrote a letter to the Wall Street Journal, on behalf of Canadians, apologizing for Canadian non participation.

61 Bellamy, Alex J, Griffin, Stuart, and Williams, Paul. *Understanding Peacekeeping.* Cambridge: Polity Press, 2004.

62 Steinbruner cites: Implacable as it has proved to be, this feature of weapons technology has been a major point of political dispute. In principle, of course, it would be strategically and morally preferable if the technical advantage could be made to favour defence over offence, and an intense body of opinion argues that with sufficient effort this could be achieved. The unrelenting fact, however, is that offensive application has sustained a decisive technical advantage over defensive application. No technical basis has been identified for a defensive system that could defeat an unrestrained offence so reliably that the deterrent effect could be abandoned. Practical arguments about defensive deployments have to do with the desirable mix of forces to preserve the deterrent effect rather than to replace it.

63 Steinbruner, John D. *Principles of Global Security.* Washington: The Brookings Institution. 2000.

64 Bellamy, Alex J, Griffin, Stuart, and Williams, Paul. *Understanding Peacekeeping.* Cambridge: Polity Press, 2004.

65 Ibid

66 Cooper, Robert. *The Breaking of Nation: Order and Chaos in the Twenty First Century.* Toronto: First McLellan and Stewart. 2003, 2004.

67 Cooper, Robert. "The new liberal imperialism." Observer Worldview Extra. April, 2002. Article available at: http://observer.guardian.co.uk/worldview/story/0,11581,680095,00.html

68 Ibid

69 Cooper, Robert. "The new liberal imperialism." Observer Worldview Extra. April, 2002. Article available at: http://observer.guardian.co.uk/worldview/story/0,11581,680095,00.html

70 Wright, Ronald. *A Short History of Progress.* Toronto: House of Anansi Press, 2004.

71 Rifkin, Jeremy. "The Dawn of the Hydrogen Economy." *Fueling the Future: How the Battle over Energy is Changing Everything.* Ed. Evan Solomon and Andrew Heintzman. Toronto: House of Anansi Press, 2003. 86.

72 See the Appendix for the relative portion of the debate transcript.

73 An anecdotal and quantitative example of this idea can be found in Particle Matter studies done by the US-Canada air quality agreement.

A 2004 "Progress Report" states: "Emissions from the north-eastern United States and southern Canada have an impact on $PM_{2.5}$ levels in many areas of the two countries, including as far east as Nova Scotia and New Brunswick, particularly influencing the top 25th percentile of $PM_{2.5}$ concentrations in these regions. Source-receptor analyses indicate that several areas contribute to elevated PM levels in eastern North America. These areas include, but are not restricted to: ·Air masses originating from a relatively large area from southeast Ohio to the western part of Virginia and western Kentucky to central Tennessee, which tended to result in relatively high $PM_{2.5}$ concentrations over north-eastern North America. ·The Windsor-Quebec City Corridor. ·The U.S. Midwest and Boston to Washington, D.C. corridor. ·The Ohio River Valley. ·Northern Alberta and Saskatchewan and central United States (e.g., Montana, North Dakota). ·Vancouver/Seattle, Oregon, and Northern California."

From: Canada-United States Air Quality Agreement. Progress Report 2004. Section 3: Scientific and Technical Research and Cooperation. Environment Canada.

74   This from the World Wildlife Fund: "WWF's ultimate goal is to build a future where people live in harmony with nature"

Greenpeace's rational for their quest for sustainable future: "When the last tree is cut, the last river poisoned, and the last fish dead, we will discover that we can't eat money..."

75   Though a widely stated fact, specific statements of such can be found via:

"The Nature Audit." *The World Wildlife Fund.* May 2003. World Wildlife Fund. 15 Apr. 2005. <www.wwf.ca/AboutWWF/WhatWeDo/TheNatureAudit/resources/PDF/The_Nature_Audit_PART_IV_No1_May2003.pdf>.

"The Zero Waste Initiative." *Cowichan Valley Regional District*, 2001. Cowichan Valley Regional District. 5 Mar 2005. <www.cvrd.bc.ca/html/pdf/ESNew/PDF4Zerowaste.pdf>.

The ideas of a national population using more resources than would be sustainable for the entire world's population is not limited to Canada, as such arguments have been made about the US, Australia and others first world nations.

76   CMAJ. The Kyoto Protocol: In force? *Canadian Medical Association Journal* 412 (2005):172-4.

77   "Smog Deaths expected to climb: OMA". *CBC News Online.*

June 14th, 2005. CBC News. 14 Jun. 2005. <http://toronto.cbc.ca/regional/servlet/View?filename=to-smog20050614.>

78 Kovats, R. Sari, Haines, Andrew. Global climate change and health: recent findings and future steps. *Canadian Medical Association Journal* 501 (2005): 172-4.

79 Bellamy, Alex J, Griffin, Stuart, and Williams, Paul. *Understanding Peacekeeping.* Cambridge: Polity Press, 2004.

80 "Geo-greening by Example." *Friedman, Thomas L.* March 27, 2005. The New York Times. 2 Jun, 2005. <http://www.nytimes.com/2005/03/27/opinion/27friedman.html?th&emc=th>.

81 The full report is available at:

"The Environmental Sustainability Index". Esty, Daniel C. et al. 2005. Yale University. 15 Mar. 2005. <www.yale.edu/esi>.

82 The rankings section can be found in the complete "2005 ESI":

"The Environmental Sustainability Index". Esty, Daniel C. et al. 2005. Yale University. 15 Mar. 2005. <http://www.yale.edu/esi/ESI2005.pdf>.

83 "Canada's Greenhouse Gas Inventory." *Greenhouse Gas Division, Environment Canada.* Aug, 2004. Environment Canada. 15 Aug, 2004. <http://www.ec.gc.ca/pdb/ghg/1990_02_report/1990_02_report_e.pdf>.

84 "Second Bush-Kerry debate, Town Hall format." *On the Issues.* Oct. 8, 2004. On the Issues. 18 Jan, 2005. <http://archive.ontheissues.org/Archive/Bush_Kerry_2_Energy_+_Oil.htm>.

85 "Bush Administration: Carbon Dioxide Not a pollutant." *Borenstein, Seth.* August 29, 2003. Knight Ridder News Service. 10 Feb. 2005. <http://www.commondreams.org/headlines03/0829-02.htm>.

86 Ibid

87 It seems that Bush's rhetoric is not the only thing made more prevalent by environmental redefinition. For example, it seems that the more recent smog days that have plagued the Greater Toronto Area in January and February of 2005 are not new because pollution is necessarily getting worse (though it is). The smog days in Toronto now appear in winter because the method of measurement has been modified. Previously it did not take certain variables into account, leaving the possibility that the population had been getting smog days in winter all along.

88 "U.S. Anthropogenic Greenhouse Gas Emissions by Gas, 2001."

Energy Information Administration, Emissions of Greenhouse Gasses in the United States, 2001. Washington DC, 2002.

89   Many students will know the equation for this relationship as

$$6 CO_2 + 6H_2O \rightarrow C_6H_{12}O_6 + 6O_2$$

90   "Forest Background". Global Environment Information Centre. 2005. Ministry of the Environment Japan. 23 Jul, 2005. <http://www.geic.or.jp//forest/background.htm>.

91   The simplified electrochemical reaction found in fuel cells is

$$2H_2 \rightarrow 4H^+ + 4e - \text{(Oxidation)}$$

$$O_2 + 4H^+ + 4e^- \rightarrow 2H_2O \text{ (Reduction)}$$

$$2H_2 + O_2 \rightarrow 2H_2O$$

... typically using Platinum (Pt) as a catalyst for the dissociation of hydrogen molecules (H_2) into hydrogen atoms 2H.

92   "International Natural Gas Information". *US Energy Information Administration*. 2005. US Energy Information Administration. 23 Aug, 2005. <www.eia.doe.gov/emeu/international/gas.html>.

93   "Historical Price Charts" GasBuddy.com. 2005. TorontoGasPrices.com. 24 Jul, 2005. <http://www.torontogasprices.com/retail_price_chart.aspx>.

94   "SUV registration". *US Census Bureau*. 2002. US Census Bureau. 23 Feb, 2005. <http://www.census.gov/prod/ec02/ec02tv-us.pdfl>.

95   Tierney, Christine. "World Auto View. The Detroit News Auto Insider." *Detroit News*. 28 Sep, 2004. 25 Mar, 2005 <http://www.detnews.com/2004/insiders/0410/31/b01-286632.htm>.

96   Table 2-5. "Canada's Greenhouse Gas Inventory." *Greenhouse Gas Division, Environment Canada*. Aug, 2004. Environment Canada. 15 Aug, 2004. <http://www.ec.gc.ca/pdb/ghg/1990_02_report/1990_02_report_e.pdf>.

97   Goldsmith, Rebecca. "SUV backlash in Europe gains traction." Newhouse News Service. 7 Oct, 2004.

98   And used it was, to describe the Waco summit. "Canada joins U.S., Mexico in security, trade deal" CBC News. 8 May 2005. <http://www.cbc.ca/story/world/national/2005/03/23/amigos-050323.html>.

99   The National. Canadian Broadcast Corporation. 23 Mar, 2005.

100   Bakan cites: "See, for discussion of examples, Debi Barker and Jerry Mander, "Invisible Government. The World Trade Organization:

Global Governance for the New Millennium?," San Francisco: International Forum on Globalization, October 1999; Lori Wallach and Michelle Sforza, *The WTO: Five Years of Reasons to Resist Corporate Globalization* (New York: Seven Stories Press, 2000); Derber, *People Before Profit*; Hertz, *Silent Takeover*."

101 Bakan cites: "See WTO Appellate Body report: "United States, Import Prohibition of Certain Shrimp and Shrimp Products: Recourse to Article 21.5 of the DSU by Malaysia," October 22, 2001, available at www.wto.org (doc. #01-5166)."

102 Bakan cites: "See WTO Appellate Body Report, "European Communities, Measures Affecting Meat and Meat Products," January 16, 1998, available at www.wto.org (doc# 98-0099)."

103 Bakan cites: "Examples discussed in Ralph Nader, "Notes from Nader: The Chill Factor: Consumer Safeguards Under Fire," World Trade Observer, Seattle, Wash., 1999, available at depts.washington. edu/wtohist/world_trade_obs/issue3/nader.htm."

104 Bakan, Joel. *The corporation: the pathological pursuit of profit and power.* New York: Free Press. 2004.

105 Pettigrew, Pierre S. *The New Politics of Confidence.* Trans. Phyllis Aronoff and Howard Scott. Toronto: Stoddard Publishing, 1999.

106 Friedman, Milton. The Corporation Dir. Mark Achbar, Joel Bakan, Jennifer Abbott. Big Picture Media Corporation. 2004.

107 Kennedy Jr., Robert F. Introduction. *Bush versus the Environment.* By Robert S. Devine. New York: Anchor Books, 2004.

108 Dixon, Homer "Bringing Ingenuity to energy." *Fueling the Future: How the Battle over Energy is changing everything.* Ed. Evan Solomon and Andrew Heintzman. Toronto: House of Anansi Press, 2003. 20.

Dixon cites: "Henry David Venema and Stephan Barg, "The Full Costs of Thermal Power Production in Eastern Canada" (Winnipeg: International Institute for Sustainable Development, July 22, 2003.)"

109 Green Breeze Incorporated. *The Business Case for Wind Energy.* Toronto: 2004.

110 "The Environmental Sustainability Index". Esty, Daniel C. et al. 2005. Yale University. 15 Mar. 2005. Page 7 of 63. <http://www.yale.edu/ esi/ESI2005.pdf>.

111 "List of countries by population density." The World Factbook, and US Census Bureau. 15 Jul, 2005. Wikipedia:

the Free Encyclopedia. 23 Jul, 2005. <http://en.wikipedia. org/wiki/List_of_countries_by_population_density>.

112 "Health, Safety and Environmental Vision." Copyright Stelco Inc. 2000. Steclo Inc. 14 Jul, 2005. <http://www.stelco. com/environmental/health/>.

113 "One Tonne Challenge". *Government of Canada.* 2005. Government of Canada. 29 Mar 2005. <http://www.climatechange. gc.ca/onetonne/english/>.

114 "One Tonne challenge: Why take the one tonne challenge?" *Government of Canada.* 2005. Government of Canada. 29 Mar 2005. <http://www. climatechange.gc.ca/onetonne/english/about.asp>.

115 ibid

116 "Canada's Greenhouse Gas Inventory." *Greenhouse Gas Division, Environment Canada.* Aug, 2004. Environment Canada. 15 Aug, 2004. Table 2-5. <http://www.ec.gc. ca/pdb/ghg/1990_02_report/1990_02_report_e.pdf>.

117 "Record heat, Record Bills". *The Toronto Star.* July 2005. 23 Jul, 2005. <http://www.electricityforum.com/news/jul05/Recordheathighbills. html>.

118 1) 750 * 5.0 = $ 37.50, 250 *5.8 = $14.50, 37.50 + 14.50 = $52.00 (plus tax)

2) 750 *5.0 = $37.50, 1250 *5.8 = 72.5, 37.50 +72.50 = $110.00 (plus tax).

119 "One Tonne Challenge Tips Brochure". Government of Canada. 2005. Government of Canada. 22 Jun, 2005. <http://www.climatechange. gc.ca/onetonne/english/OTCTipsGuide-e2.pdf>.

120 Table S-1. Page 23 of 273. "Canada's Greenhouse Gas Inventory." *Greenhouse Gas Division, Environment Canada.* Aug, 2004. Environment Canada. 15 Aug, 2004. <http://www.ec.gc. ca/pdb/ghg/1990_02_report/1990_02_report_e.pdf>.

Canada's Greenhouse Gas Inventory is a dependable source of informa-tion due to the fact that it is an official report of Canada's Greenhouse Gas emissions made to the United Nations under the United Nations Framework Convention on Climate Change (UNFCC 1992). The re-porting guidelines and methods of measurement were all either deter-mined or endorsed by the UNFCC, ensuring their objectivity, i.e. the methods were not constructed by the government of Canada.

121 "Ottawa, Carmakers reach Kyoto deal." CBC News. 6 Apr, 2005.

CBC News. 12 Apr, 2005. <http://www.cbc.ca/story/canada/national/2005/03/23/car-emissions040323.html>.

122   Ibid

123   Table A13-1: Electricity Generation and GHG emission Details in Canada. Page 261 of 273. "Canada's Greenhouse Gas Inventory." *Greenhouse Gas Division, Environment Canada*. Aug, 2004. Environment Canada. 15 Aug, 2004. <http://www.ec.gc.ca/pdb/ghg/1990_02_report/1990_02_report_e.pdf>.

124   Ibid.

125   Bakan, Joel. *The corporation: the pathological pursuit of profit and power.* New York: Free Press. 2004. Pg. 46.

       Citing: Sir John Browne, "Mobility and Choice" ("explore," "drive"); "International Relations" ("captive").

126   "Project Green." *Government of Canada*. 2005. Government of Canada. 29 Jun, 2005. Page 19 of 55. <http://www.climatechange.gc.ca/kyoto_commitments/report_e.pdf>.

127   The mechanism includes a 15$ fine per tonne of CO_2 equivalent that an emitter goes over their individual goal.

128   "Project Green." *Government of Canada*. 2005. Government of Canada. 29 Jun, 2005. Page 7 of 55. <http://www.climatechange.gc.ca/kyoto_commitments/report_e.pdf>.

129   In a 2004 ranking of OCED, including Russia, countries, and their most prominent power companies with respect to environmental sustainability, the World Wildlife Fund Ranked Hydro Quebec 4th, and the Ontario Power Generation 48th, out of a sample of 72 companies.

       "Ranking Power: Scorecards Electricity Companies." Graus, Wina, Voogt, Monique, and Langeraar, Jan Willem. November 2004. World Wildlife Fund, Powerswitch Campaign. 10 Jan, 2005. <http://www.panda.org/downloads/climate/globalranking.doc>.

Appendix:

GIBSON: Mr. President, the next question is for you, and it comes from James Hubb over here.

HUBB: Mr. President, how would you rate yourself as an environmentalist? What specifically has your administration done to improve the condition of our nation's air and water supply?

BUSH: Off-road diesel engines – we have reached an agreement to reduce pollution from off-road diesel engines by 90 percent.

I've got a plan to increase the wetlands by 3 million. We've got an aggressive brown field program to refurbish inner-city sore spots to useful pieces of property.

I proposed to the United States Congress a Clear Skies Initiative to reduce sulfur dioxide, nitrogen oxide and mercury by 70 percent.

I have – was fought for a very strong title in the farm bill for the conservation reserve program to set aside millions of acres of land to help improve wildlife and the habitat.

We proposed and passed a healthy forest bill which was essential to working with – particularly in Western states – to make sure that our forests were protected.

What happens in those forests, because of lousy federal policy, is they grow to be – they are not – they're not harvested. They're not taken care of. And as a result, they're like tinderboxes.

And over the last summers I've flown over there. And so, this is a reasonable policy to protect old stands of trees and at the same time make sure our forests aren't vulnerable to the forest fires that have destroyed acres after acres in the West.

We've got a good, common-sense policy.

Now, I'm going to tell you what I really think is going to happen over time is technology is going to change the way we live for the good for the environment.

That's why I proposed a hydrogen automobile – hydrogen-generated automobile. We're spending $1 billion to come up with the technologies to do that.

That's why I'm a big proponent of clean coal technology, to make sure we can use coal but in a clean way.

I guess you'd say I'm a good steward of the land.

The quality of the air's cleaner since I've been the president. Fewer water complaints since I've been the president. More land being restored since I've been the president.

Thank you for your question.

GIBSON: Senator Kerry, minute and a half.

KERRY: Boy, to listen to that – the president, I don't think, is living in a world of reality with respect to the environment.

Now, if you're a Red Sox fan, that's OK. But if you're a president, it's not.

Let me just say to you, number one, don't throw the labels around. Labels don't mean anything.

I supported welfare reform. I led the fight to put 100,000 cops on the streets of America. I've been for faith-based initiatives helping to intervene in the lives of young children for years. I was – broke with my party in 1985, one of the first three Democrats to fight for a balanced budget when it was heresy.

Labels don't fit, ladies and gentlemen.

Now, when it comes to the issue of the environment, this is one of the worst administrations in modern history.

The Clear Skies bill that he just talked about, it's one of those Orwellian names you pull out of the sky, slap it onto something, like "No Child Left

Behind" but you leave millions of children behind. Here they're leaving the skies and the environment behind.

If they just left the Clean Air Act all alone the way it is today, no change, the air would be cleaner that it is if you pass the Clear Skies act. We're going backwards.

In fact, his environmental enforcement chief air-quality person at the EPA resigned in protest over what they're doing to what are calling the new source performance standards for air quality.

They're going backwards on the definition for wetlands. They're going backwards on the water quality.

They pulled out of the global warming, declared it dead, didn't even accept the science.

I'm going to be a president who believes in science.

GIBSON: Mr. President?

BUSH: Well, had we joined the Kyoto treaty, which I guess he's referring to, it would have cost America a lot of jobs.

It's one of these deals where, in order to be popular in the halls of Europe, you sign a treaty. But I thought it would cost a lot – I think there's a better way to do it.

And I just told you the facts, sir. The quality of the air is cleaner since I've been the president of the United States. And we'll continue to spend money on research and development, because I truly believe that's the way to get from how we live today to being able to live a standard of living that we're accustomed to and being able to protect our environment better, the use of technologies.

GIBSON: Senator Kerry, 30 seconds.

KERRY: The fact is that the Kyoto treaty was flawed. I was in Kyoto, and I was part of that. I know what happened. But this president didn't try to fix it. He just declared it dead, ladies and gentlemen, and we walked away from the work of 160 nations over 10 years.

You wonder, Nikki, why it is that people don't like us in some parts of the world. You just say: Hey, we don't agree with you. Goodbye.

The president's done nothing to try to fix it. I will.

GIBSON: Senator Kerry, the next question is for you. It involves jobs, which is a topic of the news today. And for the question, we're going to turn to Jane Barrow.

Note: That is it. The entire extent of the environmental policy debate in the US election campaign lasted 4 minutes.